Can Legal Weed Win?

The publisher and the University of California Press Foundation gratefully acknowledge the generous support of the Barbara S. Isgur Endowment Fund in Public Affairs.

Can Legal Weed Win?

THE BLUNT REALITIES OF CANNABIS ECONOMICS

Robin Goldstein and Daniel Sumner

UNIVERSITY OF CALIFORNIA PRESS

University of California Press
Oakland, California

© 2022 by Robin S. Goldstein and Daniel A. Summer
First paperback printing 2023
Library of Congress Cataloging-in-Publication Data

Names: Goldstein, Robin (Robin S.), 1976– author. | Sumner, Daniel A.
    (Daniel Alan), 1950– author.
Title: Can legal weed win? : the blunt realities of Cannabis economics /
    Robin Goldstein and Daniel Sumner.
Description: Oakland, California : University of California Press,
    [2022] | Includes bibliographical references and index.
Identifiers: LCCN 2021045185 (print) | LCCN 2021045186 (ebook) |
    ISBN 978052097378 (paperback) | ISBN 9780520383272 (ebook)
Subjects: LCSH: Marijuana industry—Economic aspects—California. |
    Marijuana industry—Law and legislation—California. | Marijuana—
    Law and legislation—California.
Classification: LCC HD9019.M382 U625 2022 (print) | LCC HD9019.
    M382 (ebook) | DDC 338.1/737909794—dc23/eng/20211006
LC record available at https://lccn.loc.gov/2021045185
LC ebook record available at https://lccn.loc.gov/2021045186

Manufactured in the United States of America

31 30 29 28 27 26 25 24 23
10 9 8 7 6 5 4 3 2

Contents

Preface

Fear and Stoning in Las Vegas

Las Vegas, Nevada, December 2019. At the weed industry's biggest conference of the year, MJBizCon (Figure 1), hundreds of white male investors in suits are pacing around angrily. Many of the investors have lost most of the money they ever invested in weed. A major cannabis stock index has fallen 80 percent in 2019. California's legal weed market is officially "in crisis mode," according to *Marijuana Business Daily*.

At a self-styled "investor intelligence summit" preconference at the Cosmopolitan Hotel, investors and industry experts are diagnosing the disaster. Some investors blame Canadian holding companies or private equity hustlers for their woes. Others blame state governors, regulators, or stoners in the forest.

In the midst of the rubble, others claim to see a silver lining in the legal weed crisis: a new "buy-low opportunity," which has arisen from the near collapse of the market for legal weed. These fearless optimists, whose ranks include former U.S. senator Tom Daschle, a keynote speaker at MJBizCon, double down on their positions and steer others to join them. Daschle, a Democrat from South Dakota who served as U.S. Senate majority leader, is an

FIGURE 1. MJBizCon, Las Vegas, December 2019. Credit: Marijuana Business Daily / Soliman Productions.

adviser to and shareholder in Northern Swan Holdings, a multinational weed cultivator with offices in New York, Toronto, Bogotá, and Frankfurt that raised about $100 million in venture capital.

Joining Daschle in the ranks of top U.S. government leaders-turned-cannabis entrepreneurs (or lobbyist cheerleaders, depending on how much of their own pensions you think they planted to weed) is John Boehner. Boehner, from the other side of the aisle, was a Republican congressman from Ohio who served as speaker of the House from 2011 to 2015. During his career in Congress, Boehner was a steadfast and outspoken opponent of legalizing weed. Today, Boehner is on the board of Acreage Holdings, which announced a $3.4 billion acquisition deal with Canopy Growth, the world's most valuable weed company.

The weed investor optimists rely on the opinions of many industry analysts and financial reporters, who predict a major turnaround for a U.S. cannabis retail market that, in the aggregate, they see growing as large as $80 to $100 billion (on the scale of the U.S. beer market) over the next few decades.

Thomas Carlyle famously called economics "the dismal science." Economists take this mandate seriously, so the stories in this book will make it clear why we think many legal weed investors and their analysts have let the smoke get in their eyes, or at least let romantic sentiments overwhelm some simple facts and standard economic reasoning.

In many states that have fully "legalized" weed—by which we mean the introduction of state licensing, regulations, and taxes on the production and sale of "recreational" or "adult-use" weed to just about anyone 21 or over, from in state or out of state—there is now a relatively small legal weed market and a much larger illegal one.

In California, three years into the era of legalization under the Proposition 64 ballot initiative, data indicate that only about one-quarter of weed sold and consumed in the state is legally licensed and that the remaining three-quarters is produced outside legal market channels.

This dominance of illegal goods over legal ones, even well after the weed market was "legalized," should not seem surprising. Call it the economics of common sense: lower-priced sellers will win out unless the more expensive seller brings something special to the market. This rule tends to hold especially when the lower-priced option has been satisfying customers for decades.

What we have learned from our data and research over the past few years is that for the bulk of weed buyers, licensed, taxed, and regulated weed does not bring much that is special to the market—at least so far.

Legal and illegal weed look similar and have similar sensory and psychoactive qualities, but illegal weed is cheaper to produce and market than legal weed. Getting legally compliant means lots of fees; unknown, and almost always longer-than-expected, waiting periods; complex testing, tracking, packaging, and labeling requirements; and steep cannabis taxes. Staying compliant means constant monitoring to stay on the narrow course amid myriad mandates, some cannabis-specific, but many applying to any legal business. Illegal weed businesses do not face any of these costs or taxes, so they can run leaner, lower-cost operations and sell comparable products for lower prices than legal businesses can.

In our own analysis of a 2019–21 data set of more than 30 million publicly advertised U.S. retail weed prices, we are finding that prices at unlicensed weed retailers are significantly lower than prices at licensed retailers—in some states, and in some categories, as much as 50 percent lower.

Can legal weed prices ever become more sufficiently competitive with illegal weed prices?

Some costs in the legal weed market will surely fall over time as companies learn how to comply efficiently. It is possible that legal weed production might eventually reach a scale of sophistication that allows efficiencies to overcome the taxes and regulations. Such efficiencies might allow legal weed to compete on price with unlicensed cannabis. Such convergence may be happening in Colorado and Washington, where legal flower on the low end of the price scale now sells for less than $300 per pound wholesale.

However, once a producer or marketer is in the legal weed segment, governments may impose new regulatory costs or taxes on the producer at any time, as California did when it raised both its cultivation and its excise taxes in 2020. In many states, it is not clear whether the price of legal weed will ever be competitive with the price of illegal weed for most consumers. However, we think there are some regulatory steps that could help bring down the price of legal weed and make legal weed more viable in the marketplace.

The future of legal weed is uncertain. In this book we try to predict some of that future. We are not here to give investment advice, other than the advice to watch out for experts giving investment advice. We will help you understand the economics of weed, the underlying forces that are driving costs, consumer demand, and prices in the legal and illegal segments. We welcome readers to use that understanding to make their own improved judgments about the future of legal weed.

The most interesting impacts of legalization have been the most unexpected and unreported ones, and their stories are in this book: weed retail prices that have little to do with the cost of farming, heavy-duty weed investments in crisis, and laws dreamt up by activists and tech elites winding up *illegalizing* more weed businesses than they legalize. We tell the stories in plain English. We assume no background in business, economics, or statistics. We invite you, whoever and wherever you are, to come take a blunt taste of the far-out economics of legal weed.

Acknowledgments

We are deeply grateful for the guidance, editing, and support of Michelle Lipinski, Enrique Ochoa-Kaup, Tim Sullivan, Katryce Lassle, Julie Van Pelt, Teresa Iafolla, and their colleagues at UC Press who got behind our book early and led us through the publishing process with patience and skill.

We appreciate the thorough and insightful comments, criticisms, edits, and other contributions of Michael McCollough, Erick Eschker, and James Eaves on the full manuscript.

We learned so much from the people we talked to while researching this book. We thank Sabrina Fendrick, Dale Gieringer, Alexandra Stupple, Jessica Nall, Kate Devine, Aaron Smith, Sean Kelley, Richard Evans, and the many other people who graciously granted us interviews and shared their wisdom on the many aspects of cannabis about which they know much more than we do.

We thank our colleagues Bill Matthews, Jim Lapsley, Olena Sambucci, Hanbin Lee, Yolanda Pan, Hyunok Lee, Pablo Valdes-Donoso, Allie Fafard, Duncan MacEwan, Julian Alston, Phil Martin, Rachel Goodhue, Brian Wright, Rich Sexton, Jarrett Hart, Quaid Moore, Raffaele Saposhnik, Ian Xu (who helped us generate several tables and figures), and all our collaborators at UC Davis and elsewhere who worked with us to conduct the research on cannabis economics that went into this book and reviewed portions of this book.

Finally, we thank Laurie Santos, Jayson Lusk, Brad Rickard, Sue Stubbs, Barry Goldstein, and Laura Douglas for reviewing drafts of the manuscript.

Our interviewees, academic collaborators, and readers do not necessarily endorse any of the opinions or findings set forth in the book. We, the authors, take sole and complete responsibility for all factual errors, theoretical cracks, self-contradictions, botched stories, or otherwise objectionable text. We assume (and actually hope) that you, the reader, will find at least some of this book objectionable, and we thank you for your interest in reading it.

Cheers,
Robin and Dan

1   *We Call It Weed*

Weed (Figure 2) is a product of the *Cannabis sativa* or *Cannabis indica* plant that gets you high. The most common form of weed is smokable flower buds, shown in Figure 2, which you can roll into a joint or smoke from a pipe. You can also consume weed by inhaling weed vapor from an electric device, eating a weed edible, or drinking a weed tincture or beverage.

In this book, we choose to call the product "weed" rather than "cannabis" or "marijuana." In making this choice, we diverge from most of the academic literature. We prefer a term used by buyers and sellers in real markets to a term used by government regulators. "Weed" is, first of all, what most consumers call it when talking among themselves. For instance: "Does anyone have some weed?" When weed consumers say this, they mean, precisely, a product of the *Cannabis sativa* or *Cannabis indica* plant that gets you high.

Figure 3 shows the relative numbers of Google searches (in proportion to all Google searches) for the terms *cannabis*, *marijuana*, and *weed* in each calendar year between 2004 and 2020. The Y axis of the graph is a relative search volume index where 100 is set to be the maximum value. We find no evidence that the effect illustrated

FIGURE 2. Weed, in smokable flower form.

by Figure 3 can be attributed to hipsters' newfound interest in gardening.

Speaking of gardening, there's also the term *pot*, which was popular in the late 1960s through early 2000s but has been waning in popular usage in recent years; and *grass*, whose contemporary usage is largely limited to boomers.

From a market perspective, *cannabis* and *marijuana* are less precise words. *Cannabis*, although often used in regulatory language to refer to weed, technically covers a broader category of products of the *Cannabis sativa* or *Cannabis indica* plant that includes industrial hemp and smokable products that don't get you high.

Marijuana, meanwhile, is a term that was originally appropriated by the U.S. government as a slur against Mexican immigrants and was later defined under U.S. federal law as any product of the

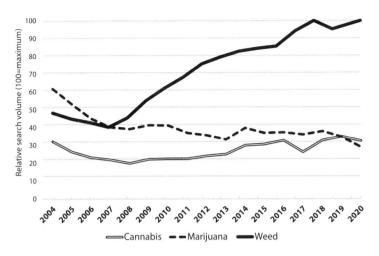

FIGURE 3. Worldwide Google search interest in "cannabis," "marijuana," and "weed."

Cannabis sativa or *Cannabis indica* plant containing more than 0.3 percent THC (tetrahydrocannabinol, thought to be the main psychoactive ingredient in weed). Thus "marijuana" technically includes forms of cannabis like hemp cloth with 1 percent THC, which you would have to be pretty desperate to try to get high on.

To confuse things further, some governments call legal weed "cannabis" and illegal weed "marijuana" or switch back and forth between terms for the legal industry. For instance, the agency that regulates weed in California was first named the "Bureau of Medical Marijuana Regulation," then renamed the "Bureau of Medical Cannabis Regulation," then renamed the "Bureau of Marijuana Control," then renamed the "Bureau of Cannabis Control," then renamed the "Department of Cannabis Control."

With due respect to the good people at these various agencies, which have been among the foremost supporters of weed economics research in the country, we just call the product "weed," whether it is legal or illegal, recreational or medical. We also encourage you to do the same when weed is what you mean.

Weed Has a Long History

Human beings have been using weed for quite a while. According to Martin Booth's *Cannabis: A History,* it was probably consumed in prehistoric civilizations for more than 5,000 years, for nutritional and perhaps also medical or spiritual reasons. Weed was "one of the first plants to be cultivated by mankind" and is now "more widely taken than any other drug save tobacco, alcohol, and aspirin."

Weed was used in Neolithic China, in Hebrew temples, by Taoist priests, and possibly by Jesus Christ. The ancient Greek historian Herodotus, in the fifth century BC, wrote of weed being part of a funeral ritual: "Transported by the fumes, they shouted in their joy." Fun funeral.

Sometime around 1155, according to Booth, in present-day northeastern Iran, a Persian monk named Haydar left his monastery near Neyshaur, went out for a walk, and discovered an unusual plant "standing unwithered by the blazing sun." Haydar "grew curious . . . so he cut a few leaves and chewed them as he went on his way. Usually a taciturn man, he returned . . . with a smile on his face" and "remained in a capricious mood until his death sixty-six years later."

As cannabis spread through the ancient world, it kept its linguistic roots in the Sanskrit *cana,* the ancient Greek *kannabis,* the Hebrew *qanneb,* Arabic *qannob,* Slavic *konopla,* Celtic *quannab,* and Spanish *cañamo.* The plant was named *Cannabis sativa* by Swedish botanist and Tree-of-Life inventor Carl Linnaeus in 1753. *Cannabis indica* was added in 1785 by Jean-Baptiste Lamarck, who identified a closely related species that was growing in India.

Although *sativa* and *indica* are thought by many in the cannabis market to have different effects on the brain, the two were long known to be hard to distinguish by their sensory or psychoactive properties. According to Booth: "It has been discovered that seeds taken from, say, a European *Cannabis sativa* plant and cultivated in India come to display some of the characteristics of the *Cannabis indica* plant in just a few generations—and vice versa."

Nowadays, there is an urban legend, supported by many budtenders across North America, that *indica* relaxes your body and puts you to sleep, whereas *sativa* makes you creative, alert, and occasionally paranoid. The *sativa-indica* divide may be an effective tool for marketing or pricing. However, we haven't seen any peer-reviewed studies showing that *sativa* could be differentiated from *indica* in a blind taste test or cognitive test, so we think that for now the issue remains unresolved scientifically.

Hemp Is Not Weed

Cannabis plants also have many industrial and standard food uses. In the United States and the rest of the world, it has long been an important agricultural crop, also known (generally when marketed in noningestible forms) as "hemp."

It is hard to infer from ancient traces of cannabis whether the plant was being ingested for its psychoactive properties, used for its fiber, or both. Hemp seed is now widely used as a food ingredient among those willing to pay high prices compared to other oil seeds. Certainly, consumers know that weed is special, whereas much cannabis (hemp) is simply practical.

Today, the distinction between "hemp" and "marijuana" is a specific legal distinction created and curated with great force by the U.S. government, which labels any ingestible *Cannabis sativa* or *Cannabis indica* products with 0.3 percent THC or less (in a lab test) as "hemp," and any products with more than 0.3 percent THC as "marijuana."

In this book, we do not include hemp when we refer to weed.

What Is Recreational Weed?

You hear a lot about recreational weed legalization. We will talk about it a lot in this book. First we ask: What does it actually mean for weed to be "recreational"?

Research and reflection suggest that the word *recreational* is a strange and vague term that people now use mostly when talking about drugs (or maybe four-wheel-drive vehicles). For drugs, *recreational* is largely used in the context of, and in opposition to, the word *medical*. The most precise way one can define the modern usage of "recreational weed" is as any legal weed that's not medical weed.

The word *recreational* has recently come into style mostly or entirely with respect to drugs, specifically as a way of referring to drugs that are not medical in the sense of having government-approved pharmaceutical uses. That is, the distinction is more a matter of law than of science or psychology.

In a former life, the Middle English word *recreation* (mental or spiritual consolation) came from the Latin *recreare* (to create again or renew), which sounds a bit like health, or at least wellness. Oxford's more modern Lexico, on the other hand, defines "recreational (adj.)" first as "relating to or denoting activity done for enjoyment when one is not working: '*recreational facilities*,'" and second as "relating to or denoting drugs taken on an occasional basis for enjoyment: 'recreational drug use.'" *Merriam-Webster,* the U.S. standard for dictionaries, goes as far as to call out Colorado weed in an example for *recreational*: "Colorado's burgeoning marijuana industry had struggled under its own astonishing success since legal recreational sales began Jan. 1."

It's a historical turn of events that "enjoyment" is now a key part of "recreational." Enjoyment, per Lexico, is "the state or process of taking pleasure in something ('the enjoyment of a good wine')." So recreation is now about pleasure, not about creation or renewal.

The Medicalization of Weed

Looking back through history, the distinctions between "food" and "drug," and between "medical" and "recreational," probably did not exist for the first few thousand years that human beings were using weed. Nonetheless, the use of weed in ways that we would now call "medical" has a long history. We can't vouch for the specific claims, but according to Booth, by the late 1800s, 50 percent of all commercial medicine was made from cannabis plants. The idea that cannabis can be medicine is nothing new, even if some (including us sometimes) roll their eyes at the labeling of stoner-paradise shops as "medical dispensaries."

Other drugs now thought of as mostly "recreational" also have histories of medical uses. Heroin was commercialized by Bayer, the pharmaceutical company, as a cure for coughs, colds, and opium addiction. Cocaine, methamphetamine (meth), and MDMA (ecstasy) also had many "medical" uses and at some points in time were administered more by doctors than by private citizens. Lately, there has also been some discussion of medical uses of psychedelics such as psylocibin (mushrooms).

Under the prevailing framework in the broad market for ingestible products (including foods, beverages, tobacco, legal and illegal drugs, etc.), all consumption is classified as either medical or recreational, and never as both—even if the medical and recreational versions of a product are identical in their physical properties. "Medical" activities are necessary measures taken in the name of personal health, hygiene, or your ability to work. In some states, medical weed users are entitled to buy and possess a substantially higher amount of weed—in California, for instance, medical weed users can possess 8 ounces, whereas recreational users can possess only 1 ounce.

Some North American values have endured since colonial Puritan days, like the idea that it is more honorable to be working than recreating. In this usage, work is whatever you earn money from doing—the production of goods and services that people are willing to pay for and want to exchange—and recreation (or leisure) is whatever you don't earn money from doing, like parenthood (unless you're Jamie Spears or LaVar Ball).

For some medicines, no legal recreational possession at all is allowed because the substances have no approved recreational use. Examples of medical-only drugs are amphetamines like Adderall (which is legal only as an attention-deficit medication) and opiates like Oxycontin (which are legal only as pain medications). Adderall and Oxycontin have total recreational prohibitions and no legal North American recreational market. The only legal use is medical use.

On the flip side of this same framework is tobacco: the only legal tobacco use is recreational use. There's no longer any medical tobacco, despite the famous doctors' recommendations to smoke cigarettes for their health benefits, which endured until the 1950s. There is also currently no medical sherry or brandy, although these too were often recommended by doctors. All carrots are recreational too: although your doctor might tell you that carrots are part of a healthy diet, they are not recommended as a medical treatment for a specific condition. Most consumer markets, like tobacco, brandy, and carrots, are 100 percent nonmedical and thus recreational.

What about alcohol?

We find it curious that such a rigid, often artificial-seeming, distinction between medicine and recreation seems to permeate all North American laws governing psychoactive substances. In a 2007 documentary entitled *The Union: The Business behind Getting High,* the narrator asks: "Why is there a perception that healthy people are affected differently, and unable to fend off the detrimental effects [of weed], whereas a person with a lowered immune system or a terminal illness experiences none of these effects?"

One thought is that putting the word *medical* in front of a product's name makes it politically acceptable. Our modern criminal code tends to forgive the activity of relieving pain but not the activity of pursuing pleasure. Yet this forgiveness is predicated on one's subjective definition of pain. The rules about what medical conditions qualify for medical cannabis differ hugely across jurisdictions—in some places, you need to have cancer, AIDS, or glaucoma to qualify; in others, mere "fatigue" gets you a prescription.

Medical Alcohol

Fun fact: Sales of alcohol, including wine and whiskey, actually remained legal in the United States throughout Prohibition (1920–33). During Prohibition, alcohol could be legally sold by only one entity—not one business entity, but one entire politically favored industry: a group of thousands of licensed stores around the country that could continue to sell alcohol with the state's permission, even as all the previously legal and licensed package stores and taverns were shut down for 13 years.

The industry that got the special permission to ignore Prohibition laws was the pharmacy (drugstore) industry. Pharmacies were licensed to sell legal alcohol that was prescribed by doctors as medicine. For all of Prohibition, any adult could buy a bottle of whiskey legally with a doctor's prescription. This advantage was a major reason that pharmacy chains expanded dramatically during Prohibition. Here, as ever, the question of what is "medical" or "recreational" is driven more by political and economic forces than by scientific ones.

What were the economic implications of one new industry controlling legal alcohol sales, where a specific, limited group of professional guild members (doctors who wrote prescriptions and pharmacists who dispensed them), collectively, were the only channel through which alcohol could be legally distributed?

One implication was that even without collusion, the doctors and pharmacies collectively benefited, via high demand and prices, from selling lower quantities than would occur in a more typical consumer market with wider distribution and more competition. Pharmacy licenses and prescription requirements, and weed licenses and prescription requirements, are not so different from the famous cases of government-limited supply such as New York taxi medallions, which sell for hundreds of thousands of dollars, or Canadian milk quotas, where the right to operate a cow costs 30 times as much as the cow.

In some ways, the current market situation for legal weed is like the market situation in the middle of alcohol prohibition, where legal and illegal sellers of substitute goods compete side by side for business. In both cases, with costly barriers to entry and a strict and limiting set of conditions in place, the majority of volume is produced and sold outside the legal channel that gives expensive permissions to just one narrow range of specialty businesses.

During Prohibition, the price of whiskey at the drugstore, including the cost of the doctor visit and the inflated price of the prescribed booze, was much higher than the price of whiskey from the bathtub or the speakeasy. Only a minority of relatively wealthy people bought their alcohol through the narrow legal channel of drugstores, and most price-sensitive consumers instead opted to get their alcohol at the illegal shop down the street. So the illegal industry never went away but instead remained for all 13 years until repeal of Prohibition in 1933.

There were clear winners on the legal side. One big winner was Walgreens, the Chicago-based pharmacy business founded by entrepreneur Charles Walgreen, who not only sold liquor legally but also invented the soda fountain. During Prohibition, Walgreens grew from a small chain of about 20 pharmacies to a mega-chain with more than 600 locations.

Second fun fact: George Stigler, the scholar who developed the economic model of firms and industries bending regulation to their benefit, held the Charles R. Walgreen Professorship at the University of Chicago, not too far from where the first Walgreens store was established.

It's one more reminder that when you're using the words *prohibition* and *legalization*, there's always more than meets the eye.

Like the medical alcohol industry after Prohibition, the medical weed industry is now in decline. In most states that have recently legalized recreational weed, including California and Washington, the medical weed market mostly dissolved and merged into the recreational market. Most legal state-licensed dispensaries that were previously medical ultimately turned themselves into recreational dispensaries (which, in this book, we generally refer to simply as "retailers"—the word *dispensary* is mostly a vestige of the medical markets, although many recreational consumers still use it). In recreational-legalization states across the U.S., the medical weed industry has either diminished substantially or virtually disappeared.

Weed Prohibitions

For about 80 years, there was a strong and growing government resistance to the use of weed. There is still a fairly widespread official government position (as codified in the current federal U.S. schedule of illegal narcotics) that weed has no medical properties and can be used only for a form of recreation that is too harmful for society to tolerate, even in citizens' private homes.

This belief seems to have emerged in the early 1900s (in the 1800s, weed was legal almost everywhere). In the 1930s, as shown in the now-cult classic propaganda film *Reefer Madness,* the U.S. government famously spread the completely false rumor that the use of weed incited murder and rape—specifically, the murder and rape of white women by Latino men.

This belief stuck around. As recently as the 1980s, U.S. president Ronald Reagan said: "Marijuana could well turn out to be the most dangerous drug that is in use in our country today." Even so, the Reagan administration of the 1980s granted certain patients with severe illnesses the legal right to use weed as medicine.

The U.S. prohibition on weed began around the same time as the U.S. alcohol prohibition, and it started, similarly, as a state-by-state movement. Massachusetts was the first U.S. state to prohibit weed, in 1911. Another 28 states would do the same in the next two decades before the 1937 Marihuana Tax Act that started the blanket federal prohibition.

There are plenty of books about the history of weed in the United States, and this is not one of them. But one interesting tidbit from the regulatory history is that out of the first 11 states to *prohibit* weed in the early 1900s (Massachusetts, California, Maine, Wyoming, Indiana, Utah, Vermont, Colorado, Iowa, Oregon, Washington), seven of them (Massachusetts, California, Maine, Vermont, Colorado, Oregon, and Washington) were among the first 11 states to *legalize* recreational weed in the modern era that started in 2014.

California was the second state to prohibit weed after Massachusetts. California's 1913 weed prohibition came at a time when the state had otherwise been leading the country in enforcement against narcotics sale and possession generally. California had already undertaken a high-profile crackdown on opium dens, which were run by Chinese immigrants, mostly in San Francisco's Chinatown.

Dale Gieringer, weed history guru and director of California's branch of the National Organization for the Reform of Marijuana Laws (NORML), writes that by 1907, "seven years before the US Congress restricted sale of narcotics by enacting the Harrison Act, the Board of Pharmacy had engineered an amendment to California's poison laws so as to prohibit the sale of opium, morphine and cocaine except by a doctor's prescription." Gieringer notes that California was singled out by Harry Anslinger, the architect of federal weed prohibition, as a model for weed prohibition policy in all other states.

After the initial U.S. enforcement craze of the late 1930s, World War II became a distraction. Neither use of nor enforcement against weed was heavy in the postwar period, as the war heroes came back to their wives who gave birth to boomers. Then came the 1960s, boomers hit adolescence, and weed came into fashion among a generation of hippies and many others of that generation.

Enter President Richard M. Nixon, who made a public display of hating hippies almost as much as he fulminated against the African Americans and Mexican immigrants with whom weed had been associated in a previous generation. In 1970, President Nixon signed the Controlled Substances Act. (For more on Nixon's deep motives, see John Ehrlichman's comments to *Harper's* in the April 2016 article "Legalize It All.")

Nixon had previously commissioned a report from the American Medical Association (AMA) but was unhappy with the AMA's finding that weed was essentially harmless, had medical benefits, and should not be prohibited. In direct opposition to the AMA's recommendations, the Nixon administration defiantly demanded the strongest penalties on weed possession and sale in world history, and got them written into the Controlled Substances Act.

Even as vast change has happened on the state level, the Controlled Substances Act has remained federal law since Nixon, and weed has remained a Schedule I narcotic, the act's most dangerous illegal drug classification—including during the Obama administration, under a president who made no secret of his youthful drug use.

The Nixon administration's strategic use of U.S. international policy also led many other countries to prohibit weed for fear of U.S. sanctions. More recent U.S. administrations have continued to use the threat of sanctions as a way of strong-arming other countries into prohibiting weed, although the Netherlands, at least, seems to have survived unscathed. But in every discussion about drug policy, the Netherlands has always been an outlier. (See the "Weed, Tobacco, and Alcohol" section below for a further discussion of Dutch coffeeshops.)

Today, legal (or illegal) weed regimes vary dramatically between jurisdictions around the world. Over time, some countries, particularly in Asia—often as part of broader overall tough-on-crime initiatives—have ended up taking weed prohibition far more seriously than Nixon ever did.

Laws in Asian countries that were first passed reluctantly in the 1970s look like they may now remain in place and continue to be harshly enforced for years after weed laws are relaxed or even eliminated in large parts of North America and some European countries. People have been executed, by firing squad, for possession of weed in Thailand and China.

And then there is Malaysia. Imagine a Californian who boarded a Malaysian Airlines flight with a bag containing a 7-ounce (200-gram) package of weed, an amount of flower that is legal for a medical cardholder to possess in California. If the bag were searched and that weed were discovered by airport authorities in Kuala Lumpur after landing, the traveler could be sentenced to death by hanging. About 150 people have been hanged for weed offenses in Malaysia.

Although the U.S. prohibition has never included the death penalty for weed possession, millions have been locked up. Under mandatory minimum sentencing policies or "three strikes and you're out" laws, hundreds of thousands were imprisoned for decades, or even for life, for repeat offenses of weed possession.

Of course, these arrests and sentences have not been doled out evenly by race, national origin, or wealth. Far from it. Across the

United States, for nearly a century, since the days when weed was first renamed "marijuana" by the government to stoke racist fears, Black and Latino people have been imprisoned for weed offenses in far greater numbers, per capita, than white people. A major reason that the weed legalization movement finally gained steam in the early 2000s was the increasingly widespread recognition of the disproportionate impact that weed prohibition has had on the Black and Latino communities for so many decades.

The Birth of the North American Legal Weed Market

From 1970, when Nixon's Controlled Substances Act went into effect, until 1996, weed was illegal everywhere in the United States, Canada, and Mexico. It was generally sold by the "eighth" (⅛ ounce) of flower (and probably some residual stems and seeds) in plastic baggies. Most suppliers delivered the weed to their customers by car. In more urban areas, some worked on foot, selling weed on streets or in parks.

In 1996, California became the first state in America to legalize the noncriminal cultivation, sale, and possession of some forms of weed, for some people, under state law. California did this by passing a ballot measure called Proposition 215, the Compassionate Use Act. Under Prop 215, weed could be legally bought, possessed, and consumed in California by any state resident over the age of 18 with a doctor's "recommendation" that lasted a full year. Weed activists celebrated not only in California but all over the world.

What was permitted under Prop 215 was only "medical" or "medicinal" weed, meaning weed that was provided to California residents who had a doctor's letter recommending weed as medicine for a diagnosed medical condition on a (long and vague) accepted list of conditions. For anyone without a doctor's letter or anyone from out of state, growing, selling, or possessing weed remained a California crime.

In the years that followed, as the medical weed movement picked up steam around the United States, California's in-state-only, doctor's-letter-only rules would become blueprints for other states' medical weed systems. Oregon, Washington, and Alaska legalized medical weed in 1998; Maine in 1999; Colorado, Nevada, and Hawaii in 2000; and 10 more states over the next 12 years. By 2012, 18 states had legalized some form of medical weed. Around the country, these bills were widely viewed as great leaps forward for the weed tolerance movement in America (Figure 4).

From the beginning, medical weed recommendations were different from medical prescriptions. Medical prescriptions are highly regulated. Medical weed recommendations, in general, have not been. In most but not all states with medical weed, the definitions of symptoms are flexible and loose. No prescription for a specific dosage is generally required, and the medical prescription delivery system used for other medicines is generally not involved in the weed market.

Another thing that many state medical weed systems had in common during the prerecreational era was that medical weed growers, suppliers, and marketing businesses were mostly unregulated by the state. In most states with medical weed, including California, there were no state licenses or state permissions needed to be a medical weed producer or seller, no special cannabis taxes, no special safety regulations; you just had to follow the rules about selling to eligible customers. The only tricky part, for some, was obtaining the local licenses or following the local regulations that some municipalities and counties imposed.

FIGURE 4. Protesters marching for legalization in Michigan. Credit: Susan Montgomery / Shutterstock.com.

In California, by 2006—10 years after passage of the Compassionate Use Act—there were medical weed dispensaries across just about every city and county in the state and weed doctors to dole out recommendations to any paying California resident. Anyone with a California ID could get a recommendation online in less than 10 minutes for about $30. After 10 more years, in 2016, when we started working with the California Bureau of Cannabis Control, we identified more than 3,000 medical dispensaries listed in California on the e-commerce portal Weedmaps.

But by 2016, California, in spite of its early adoption of medical weed, was no longer on the cutting edge of the U.S. legal weed industry. California had been leapfrogged by other states in legalizing the sale of recreational weed to all people 21 or over, including out-of-state residents. In 2012, Colorado and Washington became

Big Weed versus Big Pharma

With legalization, the weed industry has broadened its consumer reach, and new users in many age groups, some who had an earlier experience with illegal weed, have discovered medical uses for weed. Professionals in their 30s are saying, "For the first time I'm able to manage my PMS or menstrual cramps." Soccer moms and dads in their 40s are saying, "Yeah, I'm taking these new pills for my migraines, and I just gave gummies to your auntie for her back pain."

Many of these people, before discovering medical weed, had been treating their conditions with heavy doses of many different products, not getting much better yet feeling dependent on standard pharmaceuticals. The uninsured (or less-than-fully insured) among them were spending enormous amounts on medicines to manage pain. Some of these people are replacing whole medicine cabinets full of pills with baggies full of weed.

The rise of medical weed and its many uses threatens the pharmaceutical industry, which has strongly favored weed prohibitions since their very beginning in the early 1900s. Big pharma got a big boost from Nixon's Controlled Substances Act of 1970, when the U.S. imposed sanctions on trading partners that did not prohibit weed as well as some other drugs like LSD and mushrooms.

Following a trail blazed by the famed economist George Stigler's Nobel-winning contributions, economics has long looked to incentives to explain many disparate business practices, including advocacy efforts and lobbying. Two obvious long-standing economic facts that increase incentives for the pharmaceutical industry to keep weed illegal are that (1) it's generic, and no one has a patent on the *Cannabis sativa* or *Cannabis indica* species as a whole; (2) for many patients, it may be the single drug they use to treat all of their problems. People might use it for nausea, PTSD, Crohn's disease, arthritis, and cancer.

Pharmaceutical firms make money by selling a variety of expensive drugs, each with specific prescribed uses, with patients coming back again and again to doctors to get new prescriptions for different drugs for many different conditions. Many symptoms of many conditions are similar, like nausea, chills, fever, sweating, vomiting, diarrhea, and general pain. There might be thousands of distinct and important diseases, but there are really only a few dozen symptoms suffered by most patients.

We must be very clear here. Neither Robin nor Dan has any medical or pharmaceutical expertise, and we neither make nor endorse any medical or health claims of any drug, including weed. But what is clear is that the proposition of medical weed is broad. A medical practitioner might say: "You can just take pills or edibles or smoke it or dab it or vaporize it, but you are using the same natural agricultural product (and active ingredient) to treat what ails you." Nobody has figured out a way to patent a generic weed gummy, a weed cookie, or weed flower. Thus legal weed can threaten a chunk of pharmaceutical demand. Nonetheless, the pharmaceutical industry did not stop medical weed or force weed to be identified solely as a recreational product akin to beer. The medical weed enthusiasts before 1996 seem to have flown under the corporate political radar until it was too late.

Well into the 1990s, medical weed was still just about as, um, grassroots as a movement can get. It was basically weed growers and people who used the stuff medicinally, followed by a bunch of people who liked to smoke weed and go surfing, or just sit around with a glass of wine and a spliff. It was the schoolteacher and the tourist, the cancer patient and the jerk. Weed was just a part of so many people's lives that to ask if it was or wasn't medical was simply irrelevant.

For big pharma, on the other hand, weed's potential commercial success as a substitute "medicine" has long been the most relevant question of all.

the first two U.S. states to pass laws creating legal recreational weed markets. In both Colorado and Washington, legal recreational retail stores and delivery services opened in 2014.

California, meanwhile, had rejected an earlier proposition for legal weed in 2010. It was not until 2016 that another recreational legalization ballot measure—Prop 64—appeared on the ballot, and this one passed. Unlike the state's loose medical weed system, Prop 64 required an elaborate legal and regulatory system for the production and sale of recreational weed, including state licensing and taxation. Implementation of California's recreational weed system began in 2018, four years after the systems launched in Colorado and Washington.

Once again America's weed activists celebrated, as they had in 1996. But the stories we will tell in this book suggest that if the activists had foreseen the near future of legal weed, their celebrations might have been more muted.

We try to avoid being bound too much by the specifics of the North American weed landscape at any single point in time. The industry is evolving faster than books can keep up with. Instead we provide the background needed for understanding the economics of legalization and the implications that follow. For up-to-date information, we invite you to look up the latest maps of state and national legalization across North America, including Mexico, which at this writing was already on the road to recreational legalization.

The next chapter will take you through the life cycle of a weed market as it legalizes, thus splitting what was one fully illegal weed market into two markets that exist side by side: legal weed and illegal weed.

2 *Legal versus Illegal*

A Market Battle

Legalization Splits One Weed Market into Two

Everywhere in North America, we once had a single illegal weed market, with weed prices that varied somewhat by state. Illegal weed tended to be more expensive where antiweed enforcement was more vigorous. But then, starting in 1996, as we explained in Chapter 1, a variety of U.S. states and Canada begin legalizing weed in various ways.

In most of the places that have legalized, newly legal weed growers, manufacturers, and sellers must go through the process of entering the world of legal business. That means paying taxes, complying with labor laws and environmental regulations, and following a variety of rules that other legal businesses take for granted.

Beyond these basic burdens, for weed businesses, becoming legal means getting a state license to operate, generally getting city or county permissions, paying licensing fees and taxes, and meeting many rigorous government-imposed cannabis-specific rules. Compliance with these rules is now enforced, to varying degrees, by government agencies.

Legal Weed   Illegal Weed

FIGURE 5. Legal weed and illegal weed.

At the same time, in all of these places there is still a thriving unlicensed and illegal weed market that competes side by side with legal weed, with old-fashioned illegal weed producers operating off the radar, getting no licenses, meeting no standards, paying no taxes, and selling through traditional illegal back channels.

From the point of view of economics, in every part of North America that has introduced any form of legal weed system, weed is now divided into two markets: legal weed and illegal weed (Figure 5). Every consumer who buys weed in North America is participating in at least one of these two markets.

What's the Difference between Legal Weed and Illegal Weed?

From the perspective of most consumers, the short answer is that there's not much difference. The products, especially in flower form, are almost identical. Here's why.

First of all, when you take some weed flower out of the package, the weed inside one package looks a lot like the weed inside any other package. Experts and connoisseurs may notice myriad differences between products, but to most consumers, weed just looks like weed.

Similarly, to most consumers, one glass of red wine, after being poured, looks a lot like any other glass of red wine. Experts may be able to tell the difference between a merlot and a pinot noir from the color of the wine or its aromas, but one thing that's impossible for anyone to discriminate, just from looking at or tasting wine in the glass, is the legal status of the wine's supplier. Even the world's greatest wine critic couldn't tell, from drinking a glass of red wine, whether its importer has a valid license from the U.S. government.

Likewise, even the world's greatest weed critic, if handed a bud, wouldn't be able to tell—from the taste of the smoke or its effects on the body—whether the weed's producer and seller have a state license in good standing. Anyone would need to see the package or know where the weed came from in order to differentiate legal weed from illegal weed. The difference between legal and illegal weed is purely nonsensory information.

Another thing to keep in mind is that when you have recreational legalization, it's not a crime for a consumer to buy or smoke illegal weed. It's only a crime to sell illegal weed. So there's no difference for the consumer from the perspective of legal risk. Consumers, from the start, have no particular incentive to favor legal weed.

Consumers' only incentive, as when they choose between brands of eggs, is to buy the product (and associated services) with the best price-quality combination they can find—legal or illegal. Quality matters to consumers, but so does price. Every consumer has a different definition of quality. So in the end, some consumers will buy legal weed, others will buy illegal weed, and still others will sample both and participate in both markets, buying some legal weed and some illegal weed.

For the market story we tell in this chapter, we limit the discussion to smokable flower, which looks something like the weed in Figure 5. We'll set aside vape pens, gummies, brownies, tinctures, wax, shatter, and other products, although the same general principles apply to those categories too.

How Do You Choose between Legal Weed and Illegal Weed?

Every consumer is an individual. Every consumer has unique beliefs, desires, likes, and dislikes that are different from every other consumer's. Whoever you are, your choice between legal and illegal weed depends on a complex set of factors including the circumstances of the purchase, the price, the quality, and so on, measured against your own unique set of preferences.

We treat weed attributes such as convenience, perceived safety, and social acceptability of buying from one market versus the other as attributes that are valued by consumers in an individual way, not a universal way. Among some consumers who have been buying illegal weed for decades, the idea of walking into a store and buying from a licensed seller might just seem odd. Among other consumers, buying illegal weed might be considered morally wrong. Every consumer has a choice between the two and will use personal preferences to make the choice.

For almost every consumer, price also matters in that choice.

Let's say that back in the day when all weed was illegal, you were spending an average of $25 per eighth (⅛ ounce of smokable weed flower) for your usual illegal weed delivery from your trusted guy who knows a guy. Now, after legalization, you face a choice between sticking with your old illegal weed delivery service and switching to a legal weed delivery service that's selling a very similar product.

If illegal weed were going to be delivered to your door in 10 minutes and cost you $25 per eighth, and legal weed were going to take several hours and cost you $50 per eighth, then unless you were very rich and very patient, you might find it hard to justify ditching illegal weed for legal weed.

Even if legal and illegal weed cost the same, were of the same quality, and were delivered in the same amount of time, you might have plenty of reasons beyond price not to switch to legal. Maybe you like the illegal weed you are used to smoking, you know who grows it, and you think the price is fair. Maybe you are buying from friends you care about, and you want to keep supporting their livelihoods. Maybe you enjoy being slightly rebellious and buying something underground.

On the other hand, you might also have some reasons to switch to legal weed, even if it costs more. It's certified as pesticide-free; it has THC, CBD, and other measurements printed on the label; and it probably comes in a nicer package, suitable for gifting. Some consumers are clearly willing to pay extra for such safety, information, and beauty attributes.

As the legendary economist Thorstein Veblen liked to point out, preferences can also include "social signaling" or "conspicuous consumption," that is, the desire to impress others with one's purchases. Your choice between legal and illegal weed could have social dimensions. Depending on your crowd (or which party you're showing up at), legal weed might be cooler or less cool than illegal weed.

The Substitution Effect

To sum up what we've said so far, legal weed and illegal weed are competing side by side for consumer dollars with products that are very similar from the perspective of most consumers. Some consumers are willing to pay a lot more for legal weed, some are willing to pay a little more, some aren't willing to pay any more, and some are even willing to pay more for illegal weed. In economics, we would therefore say that legal weed and illegal weed are close "substitutes" in the market sense, even if they are not substitutes for some buyers.

When we call product A and product B substitutes, we mean, generally, that an increase in the price of product A relative to the price of product B will result in a decrease in the number of units of A demanded. This is because as the relative price of A rises, some consumers will buy less of A and more of B because of its comparatively better value.

For instance, in the latte-to-go market, Starbucks and Peet's Coffee are substitutes. They offer similar products in similar environments. Currently their latte pricing is similar. Let's say it's around $4 per latte. Similar prices are a hallmark of competitive markets with different sellers offering close substitute goods. If Starbucks raises its price per latte to $8 while Peet's keeps its price at $4 in the same neighborhood, a lot of Starbucks customers will switch to Peet's. The increase in the quantity demanded at the local Peet's is the substitution effect.

Legal weed and illegal weed, like Starbucks and Peet's, are close, competitive substitutes. Each may have its pros and cons even if the price differs, because they are not identical. Products (and the services that go with them) do not need to be identical to be substitutes.

Supply, Demand, and Weed

Weed is like many other consumer products—eggs, milk, cigarettes, bacon, and more. It starts on a farm somewhere; goes through a few production stages (the supply side); then goes through some processing, packaging, and marketing stages; and finally gets to a consumer (the demand side). Where we draw the line between the supply side and the demand side depends on which stage along the market channel we focus on.

Let's start at the end rather than the beginning. Consider weed that is sold to consumers at a retail store in Oklahoma. In this case, everything that comes before the consumer, including the product flow from producers to wholesalers, and wholesalers to retailers, is "supply," and only the consumers represent "demand."

Given that this book includes "economics" in its title, it would be false advertising not to include at least one supply-and-demand chart within its pages. We will show you three to illustrate some simple concepts about legal and illegal weed. We will keep the pictures abstract.

We think it's worthwhile to go through the chart slowly the first time and then just jump into the substance in the next ones. (If this supply-and-demand stuff is trivially obvious to you, or on the flip side if you don't have the patience for this more technical material, you can skim it or skip ahead to the next section, but you will miss the fun.)

In the illustration we consider the demand for weed by buyers in Oklahoma and the supply of weed from those who sell in the retail market in Oklahoma. We chose Oklahoma as our example because Robin thinks roses are pretty.

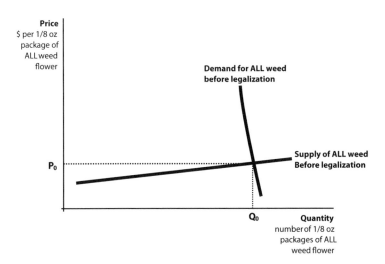

FIGURE 6. Supply and demand for retail weed in Oklahoma (including legal and illegal weed).

Figure 6 shows a stylized hypothetical supply and demand diagram for weed. The horizontal axis represents the total quantity (amount, in pounds) of weed sold in Oklahoma. To be concrete, we represent all weed in ⅛-ounce flower package equivalents of some standardized quality. Here we are talking about *all* weed, legal or illegal. (This choice of a specific unit and a specific representative product is not trivial, but using ⅛-ounce flower packages alone is much easier than, for example, converting all greenhouse gases into carbon dioxide equivalents—and the fate of the planet does not hinge on getting this exactly right.)

The vertical axis represents how much money buyers pay and what sellers receive for each ⅛-ounce package. The units are ⅛-ounce packages of a certain standardized quality of weed, and the price of those packages represents in a simple way the wide variety of products in the complicated real-world market for all weed.

Although legal and illegal weed are close substitutes, there are few close substitutes for weed *as a whole*. Most weed is sold to people who consume weed regularly, and evidence from around the world suggests that people who consume regularly don't smoke substantially more or less weed when the price of weed changes. We expect that most weed buyers in Oklahoma, like Willie Nelson, Snoop Dogg, and most other weed buyers in the world, will buy and smoke about the same total amount of weed (legal plus illegal combined) regardless of what it costs (within some realistic range). To reflect this expectation, we drew the demand curve for *all* weed as (in economic terms) very "inelastic," meaning an almost vertical line with a very steep slope.

The supply curve for all weed, on the other hand, is very elastic. The supply curve in Figure 6 slopes up only a little and is nearly horizontal, because getting a lot more weed to Oklahoma buyers costs only a bit more *per unit*. Oklahoma suppliers can get more weed to the market pretty quickly with little extra expense. Indoor growers and greenhouses produce weed year round. Weed does not use much land or many other specialized inputs that would make the price jump when more is produced. And weed does not grow on trees, meaning that we don't have wait five years for the tree to grow to get more weed. Equally important, for the very elastic supply of *all* weed, is the fact that weed from lots of other places (California, Colorado, and others) crosses the porous border to satisfy Oklahoma consumers, who account for just 1 or 2 percent of U.S. consumption.

Figure 6 shows that the demand and supply curves cross at price P_0 and quantity Q_0. Figure 6 helps us "visualize" that if weed gets more costly to produce or market (meaning the whole supply curve shifts up), people still get their weed, but they have to pay more. The price must rise enough keep the weed supply coming. When the price rises a lot, the quantity demanded falls just a little bit, because buyers want their weed no matter what. That is also what happens with eggs, bacon, cigarettes, and many other farm products in the consumer market, and it is particularly characteristic of drugs, such as bacon, that are thought to be at least somewhat addictive. Similarly, if weed gets more popular in Oklahoma (the demand curve shifts out), the quantity of weed consumed will rise, but the price goes up only a little. Suppliers find it easy to get more weed to Oklahoma buyers at little extra expense per unit.

But Figure 6 has a problem: it is not of much use for the purpose of this book, which is to consider the impacts of legalization and the market for *legal* weed. Figure 6 treats all weed as though it all had comparable costs of production and marketing, and that is just not right.

So next let's consider only the *legal* weed price and quantity when we start from the *all*-weed price of P_0 and the all-weed quantity of Q_0. The first thing to note is that weed, to be legal, must comply with a series of regulations, none of which are free. Furthermore, legal weed suppliers must pay taxes that illegal weed ignores. Most regulations and taxes apply to all legal businesses, not just legal weed. Weed taxes and regulations are a big deal even in business-friendly Oklahoma, although not nearly as costly as in states like California or Massachusetts.

Figure 7 illustrates what happens when suppliers of legal weed pay taxes and regulation costs on every unit of legal weed sold in Oklahoma: the untaxed and unregulated weed has a different set of (lower) costs. The vertical distance from the supply curve before legalization to the supply curve labeled legal weed is just the cost of taxes and regulations built into each ⅛ ounce of legal weed.

What is the demand situation for legal weed when unlicensed and untaxed illegal weed is available in Oklahoma as a substitute? Weed consumers in Oklahoma now have a choice between buying weed through two different market segments. Of course, the products, sales venues, variety, and selection may differ between legal and illegal. But weed consumers find weed available from both sets of sellers.

Just like shoes, weed is now available from a variety of sellers who compete for customers. Some people prefer buying weed from the legal, tax-paid, regulated segment. They may like the nice store or the safety-tested products. Or they may just like the idea that the transaction is legal. Other buyers may prefer to get weed from the same guy who has always sold them weed and who may not have great variety but has what his customers want. Some buyers might not care very much whether the weed they buy is legal or illegal, while other buyers might care a lot.

In this situation, we treat legal weed and illegal weed as *substitutes* in demand.

The demand curve for legal weed in Figure 7 is downward-sloping but pretty flat because legal weed now has a good economic substitute in the overall weed market. Buyers do not cut back much on weed when the overall weed price rises. But when the price of legal weed is a lot higher than the price of illegal weed because of the taxes and regulations, many consumers stay with the illegal segment, and legal weed consumption is much smaller than it would otherwise be. That does not mean Oklahoma consumers give up weed—it means they continue to buy illegal weed.

In Figure 7, the price of legal weed is high because of taxes and regulations, and the quantity of legal weed is low because a cheap substitute, illegal weed, is still available. In Figure 7, illegal weed is offstage but is dominating the action.

Figure 8, on the other hand, shows the action in the *illegal* weed segment. The supply of illegal weed is still flat and the supply curve does not shift. No taxes or regulatory costs are added on the supply side of illegal weed. Illegal weed growers and processors try to stay off the grid and out of sight. But the demand for illegal weed is now also flat and shifts back a bit because, when the legal weed market opened, a new substitute way to get weed became available.

The shift back in the demand labeled *illegal* weed in Figure 8 is just the reflection of the quantity of demand for *legal* weed in Figure 7. Total weed sold in Oklahoma may not change much, but now illegal weed quantity is a bit lower and its price may fall a little with the new competition.

As we emphasize throughout this book, understanding the role of illegal weed in the market, and the effect of illegal weed on the prices and quantities of legal weed, is a major topic for economists studying weed markets. One way to stimulate legal weed sales and revenue would be to attract customers away from the illegal sellers, and one way to do *that* would be with low taxes and looser legal weed regulations that would lower the price and increase the availability of legal weed. For example, Oklahoma, despite legalizing only medical weed, has allowed many retail licensees and an especially vibrant retail market for legal weed.

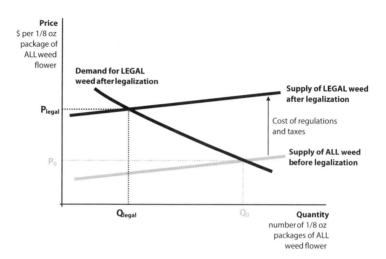

FIGURE 7. Supply and demand for legal retail weed in Oklahoma (not including illegal weed).

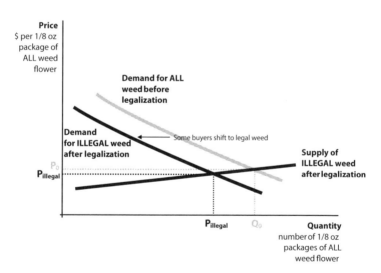

FIGURE 8. Supply and demand for illegal retail weed in Oklahoma (not including legal weed).

Another way to shift business to the legal weed segment is for law enforcement to attack the illegal weed segment with great vigor in an attempt to raise the costs of illegal suppliers. Raising the cost of supplying illegal weed (meaning the supply curve in Figure 8 would shift up vertically) would force the price of illegal weed to rise. Therefore, the quantity of illegal weed demanded would fall. If the price of illegal weed went up, back in Figure 7, because the substitute became expensive, the demand for legal weed would shift out and more legal weed would be demanded.

Frankly, it is not clear that governments are willing or able to impose large new costs on sellers of illegal weed, so this enforcement option seems limited.

As long as legal weed remains expensive and highly regulated, and many buyers continue to find illegal weed a good alternative compared with illegal weed, the legal weed segment will continue to be severely limited in its potential to get big. Next, in Chapter 3, we will move from the abstract to the concrete and get down and dirty with the economic challenges now faced by legal weed.

3 *Prices Get High*

This chapter deals with simple questions. First, why is weed so expensive and legal weed far more expensive than illegal weed? And, second, even where weed is legal, why does illegal weed still seem to capture the bulk of the trade?

The questions are simple. The answers are not as simple, but we hope they are illuminating.

In large part because of its history of illegality, along with the taxes and regulatory costs we've discussed above, weed is orders of magnitude more valuable, by weight, than any other legal agricultural commodity. As we explain below, weed, wherever it grows and under any institutional setting, is very expensive per unit of weight, even if it's sometimes pretty cheap per unit of impact on your brain.

A typical pound of legal weed flower might leave the farm at about $1,500 per pound. That is $3 million per ton. Compare this to corn grain, which sells for less than $200 per ton; alfalfa hay, which sells for $250 per ton; or almonds, which sell for as much as $6,000 per ton—pricey by agricultural standards, but just 0.2 percent of the price per ton of weed.

Weed prices are even more impressive at retail. In a U.S. state with recreational legalization, you might pay about $45, after tax, for an eighth—or about $5,800 per pound, three times as much as white truffle or Beluga caviar—for a typical package of legal flower.

Let's say this works out to a retail price of about $35 per eighth, plus $10 in sales, excise, and local taxes. So the total is about $45, versus the $25 price of illegal flower. These aren't exact numbers, but they're on the order of what we've been observing in our data.

Why is legal weed so much more expensive than illegal weed?

The short answer is that is more costly to operate a legal weed business than an illegal one. But why is that?

Here comes the long answer. First, a quick few facts about how the cannabis industry works.

Growing Weed Is Harder Than Growing Weeds

Farming is hard. It is even harder to farm profitably. That statement applies doubly to farming weed because of the complications of being illegal that many weed farmers face—or the even larger complications of being *legal* that other weed farmers face. Legal or illegal, weed is expensive for farmers to grow and sell.

The typical marketable output from a weed farm is some THC-rich dried flower buds and some dried leaves and stems, which are less THC-rich and fetch a lower price per pound. Often the leaves and stems are pressed and distilled into THC oil.

Weed is sold by the pound, but it does not weigh much when dried, so the price per pound is high. Unlike for many crops, the land, water, equipment, and other material inputs are a small share of the cost of production. Capital and labor are the big cost items per unit of land and per pound of output.

Some commercial weed is grown in regular dirt, outdoors, under sunlight. In that situation most farms harvest one crop per year and get lower prices than indoor or greenhouse weed. Still, an acre of legal weed can cost $1 million or more to grow and earn $1 million or more of farm revenue. Obviously the outdoor climate matters, and in some places weed does poorly when grown outside.

Much weed is grown in greenhouses, with varying amounts of artificial light. Greenhouse weed farms get several harvests per year and use their space more intensively than outdoor growers. Greenhouse growers also have considerable control over the growing environment, and they achieve high yield per square foot and high THC per pound of weed. They get higher prices and usually much more revenue per acre than outside growers.

A few years ago, we did a study for a group of cut-flower farmers about competition for greenhouse space. The traditional flower farms grew products like tulips and lilies. They were worried about losing greenhouse space to the new flower farmers who grew legal weed. Cut flowers are at the high end of intensive farming, and cut-flower revenue seemed very high—about $10,000 or more in annual revenue per greenhouse.

We had to tell the good folks in the cut-flower business that any weed grower that wanted to rent a greenhouse would get it. With $1 million in annual revenue per greenhouse, a weed farmer had much more to worry about than a few hundred dollars in extra rent. Fortunately for the cut-flower club, you don't need much greenhouse space to grow all the legal weed that the market will bear, so there are still plenty of greenhouses to go around.

A lot of weed is also grown indoors under controlled conditions with expensive structures and expensive artificial light and heat.

Expensive management, elaborate technology, and even more added costs mean some indoor weed companies have made enormous capital expenditures before harvesting a single pound of weed. But for such indoor operations, weed yield is very high per square foot, and their weed commands the highest prices. So the best-managed of these investments, at least, may pay off.

Weed farming is expensive, which is the basic reason that weed will always be expensive per ton. But as we now explain, a lot of the current costs are driven by the cost of illegality on one side of the market and the cost of legality on the other side of the market.

Manufacturing Products from Weed: Value-Added, or Just Cost-Added?

Much of the overall dried cannabis flower production in North America goes directly from farm to wholesale buyers and on to retailers, which may be divisions of the same vertically integrated company. Some of the flower (likely that which is not quite suitable for retail consumers) and most of the dried leaves go to manufacturers for processing into products such as vape pens, oil cartridges, edibles, tinctures, waxes, and beverages.

Making weed products from weed flower and leaves is much like food processing. Quality dried flower is like milk, eggs, and produce that get to the grocery store looking a lot like they did when they left the farm. The manufactured products are like all the other aisles of a food store. The products look nothing like farm raw material, but the important ingredient is processed into forms of goods the consumer wants.

Weed leaves and flowers are turned into THC-rich oil and then inserted into cartridges and vape pens or some other delivery device. Alternatively, some companies just do the oil extraction and sell oil to the baker or candy maker that does the food manufacturing. A wide variety of products also deliver THC through the skin.

Many manufacturing companies do lots of fancy packaging and brand marketing in attempts to differentiate themselves from lower-priced competitors who are the generics in the business. This is another way weed is like wine. The packages themselves often differ more than what is in the package.

Legal manufacturing has another challenge: to comply with track-and-trace systems that attempt to assure that no legal weed leaks out to the illegal market and no illegal weed leaks into the legal weed market. Clearly, given the incentives, regulations mostly try to keep illegal weed from entering licensed manufacturing processes. States and provinces have elaborate systems that attempt to label every plant and then relabel every batch of weed as it is shipped from the farm (even if the shipment just goes down the hall from the grow-room to the manufacturing part of the same company).

Each licensed manufacturer must account for which batch of leaves and flowers is used for each batch of oil to ensure that no oil is made from an unlabeled pile of illegal weed. Then each batch of brownies has to be labeled with which batch of oil, and therefore which batch of weed, was used in the bakery.

Naturally, all this tracking and tracing is not free. Nor is it perfect. The price difference between legal weed at the farm and illegal weed at a different farm creates incentives to slip some illegal weed into the process despite all the costly and time-consuming labeling and recordkeeping.

Many unlicensed, illegal weed manufacturers have expanded with the rise of the legal market. They can use cheaper raw materials, take shortcuts in processing, and pay no royalties to brand owners whom they may rip off. You might be able to buy Willie Weed (packaged with a picture of an old white guy with a gray ponytail) from the guy on the street, but you can bet a dollar that Willie Nelson is not getting a penny from that dime bag.

Wholesale Services and Retailing

Nobody likes the middleman. Hardly anyone can say "marketing" without a tone of mild disdain. Even businesspeople who are proud of their marketing acumen have to practice to keep that tone out of their voice.

At the same time, we know that somebody has to do it (marketing), and it is generally the law in U.S. states and Canadian provinces that legal weed must go through a wholesale "distributor." The three-stage marketing requirement applies to weed that goes from a farm to a manufacturer, to weed that goes directly from the farm to the retailer, and to weed that goes from the manufacturer to the retailer. Every package of legal weed must go through a licensed distributor, and often it goes through a distributor several times before reaching a consumer.

A package of weed moved from a farm to a manufacturer must be officially handled by a distributor even if all three licensees are part of the same vertically integrated company, and even if the transport involved is walking down the hallway with a 20-pound package of weed. Also, any movement between two manufacturing companies—say the sale of weed oil to a bakery—must be handled by a licensed distributor. Of course, every one of these legal weed transactions or movements must be registered in the track-and-trace system.

Some distributors are independent companies that buy bulk weed and sell weed to retailers in fancy packages. Others may just provide the required transport, tax payment, and holding services for a fee. The markups of wholesalers over what they pay to farmers for weed or to manufacturers for weed products must cover the costs of whatever services the wholesaler provides.

Wholesale marketing of illegal weed is also costly. But for illegal weed, no laws, regulations, or taxes add to the cost of goods or overhead. The big added cost for illegal weed consists in avoiding the law and avoiding theft without legal enforcers to help. Wholesale marketers of illegal weed must build in costs of avoiding detection by the authorities.

The Cost of Being Legal

Now we come back to our question about the costs of legal weed versus illegal weed.

First, we want to note that running any legal business has costs that can be avoided by an illegal counterpart. There are many levels of complex and costly regulations, licensing fees, and other compliance costs simply to be a legal business in any market. Compliance is not just with unique cannabis regulations but also with the many ordinary local, state, and federal regulations, fees, and taxes that make any legal business costlier to run than underground ops at the same scale.

Workers who have done any one thing for the past 10 or 20 years have specialized skills. The skills of illegal weed workers, and especially managers, in Humboldt County, California, are particularly specialized. Humboldt County has been supplying a big chunk of the U.S. illegal weed market nationwide for many decades. The skills necessary to be an illegal Humboldt County weed grower or marketer include not only the specifics of weed farming in a cool, rainy place but also the skills of keeping under the radar from local, state, and federal law enforcement: for instance, shielding outdoor crops from satellite or helicopter detection with canopy from other plants.

Humboldt County weed execs were (and are) also skilled at finding and maintaining relationships with networks of illegal interstate transporters, some of whom were (and are) connected with drug cartels or organized crime syndicates. Illegal sellers have also become adept at dealing with the personal and financial risks of settling personal or business disputes in an outside-the-law way.

We do not want to underestimate the costs of being in an illegal cannabis business. Clearly, being (mostly) legal is appealing to most of us. The threats from law enforcement and from other businesses who are operating outside the law are costly. Most businesses in most industries find it best to remain legal. But here we emphasize that staying illegal, for those with the expertise and experience, also has some advantages.

Many illegal producers in Humboldt had little trouble getting into the unregulated medical weed market, while it existed from 1996 to 2017, as a way to sell some of their production locally and with lower business and personal risks. But selling into the unregulated prerecreational markets wasn't much different from selling illegally. Nothing about these transactions had to involve the government. Even the most "legal" of medical weed businesses in prerecreational states conducted their affairs in an informal way. Especially in the farm and wholesale market stages, most were not compliant with most ordinary state regulations or taxes, and local regulations were ad hoc and haphazardly enforced.

Many observers thought California's introduction of a legal recreational (licensed, regulated, and taxed) weed system in 2018 would help the preexisting illegal and medical weed producers by enabling them to "transition" into the legal market where they no longer had to fear the law. The mistake these observers made was assuming that people who were experienced and talented at unregulated farming, manufacturing, wholesaling, and retailing would do well at running legally licensed farms and the rest of the operations, and thus would be well positioned to easily enter the newly regulated cannabis market after legalization.

Cultivation, the process of successfully growing and harvesting plants, is an important skill. Cultivation is hard, and even small mistakes can ruin a crop, reduce yield, or compromise quality. But growing the crop is not the most important skill in running a modern crop farm business—not for alfalfa or walnuts, and certainly not for weed. Business expertise may be even more important than farm expertise.

Generally the skill set needed to run an unregulated farm or marketing business (e.g., shading fields from police helicopters, guarding suitcases of cash, and maintaining secrecy) does not translate to the skill set needed to run a legal business (e.g., filing tax returns, keeping permits up to date, and negotiating with city councils and county boards). Part of the story here is that many of the farms that supplied the legal medical weed in California for about two decades were not really operating as normal legal businesses. Most did not really know what it meant to be legal and were not well prepared for a transition.

In the case of weed, particularly rigorous compliance standards are in place across North America, whether systems have been set up by ballot propositions (as in California) or legislative acts (as in Canada). Legal weed can be sold only through a licensed retailer. Legal weed must be produced and handled only by licensed producers and distributors. Manufacturing and packaging of legal weed may occur only in licensed facilities, and every step and product transformation must be tracked and traced from "seed to sale" via a state-administered database.

In every North American legal recreational market, meticulous documentation accompanies the weed through every movement and step through the supply chain. Suppliers must often use child-proof packaging, pass rigorous safety and potency tests run on mass spectrometers by specialized state-certified cannabis testing labs, hire approved managers and security guards, run security cameras with archival storage, buy and operate state-mandated software to track inventory, follow safe waste disposal protocols, and more.

The process of becoming compliant with safety rules, environmental regulations, local zoning rules, worker insurance laws, and so on—including the cost of lawyers, consultants, and the long wait—often requires more capital than is required to build the facilities themselves. Long waits for local and state license applications to be approved are a particularly common source of capital shortfalls and investor temper tantrums. When licenses are approved, their fees can be thousands, tens of thousands, or hundreds of thousands of dollars per year. So previously operating cannabis businesses do not find it easy to shift to the legal market, and the new legal growers, processors, and retailers disappoint investors who expect huge growth and extraordinary and immediate returns.

In the preregulation legal medical weed market, the preexisting level of state oversight had often amounted to little more than a wink and a nod. Many preexisting businesses that had thrived in that prerecreational medical weed market had a really tough time entering and adjusting to the conditions in the new postrecreational weed world, just as many street weed dealers would probably have a tough time getting a job as a budtender at a legal weed shop in West Hollywood.

To open, run, and manage a legal cannabis shop in the early years of the industry requires skills that most successful business executives don't have. The first versions of state regulations usually include at least a few rules that nobody can figure out how to follow, whether a Harvard MBA, a UC Davis plant physiologist, or anyone else. Many of the rule makers and lobbyists behind weed laws around North America have never smoked or handled weed and know little about the industry. So they have often written impossible or absurd things into the law or regulations.

For example, consider an early version of a California rule (later revised) that required weed must be delivered in cargo vans. At $45 per ⅛-ounce package, a retail pound of cannabis is worth $5,760 per pound. One can easily put a million dollars' worth of cannabis in the trunk of a Honda Civic and have plenty of room to pick up the kids on the way.

Slowly over time, some of the most absurd previsions get rewritten or are left wisely unenforced by authorities. But in weed, more than in most markets, total compliance with the law is not a realistic possibility or even a known quantity. Compliance is a wish upon a star—with the addition of a never-ending, always-nerve-wracking game of regulatory risk management.

So legal weed is a difficult market for anyone to enter and a costly one to be in, and that accounts for why legal weed is much more expensive than illegal weed in most states—even before taxes.

The Risk Premium

Economists sometimes use the term *risk premium* to refer to the extra cost of operating or investing in an especially risky business. You would need to pay a lot more per hour for an arsonist than for a taxi driver. The arsonist is taking on a substantial risk of death or imprisonment and commands a premium for taking on that risk. In states such as Texas that do not yet have any functioning legal cannabis system (medical or adult-use), consumers buy their cannabis from illegal dealers, much as they have done for many decades, and pay a risk premium that is absent from the price of beer or cigarettes.

A new sort of risk premium emerges when governments legalize recreational weed and create large-scale agencies to implement and enforce new and complicated licensing rules, safety standards, and other regulations. The agency mandate is to enforce those rules on licensees: that is, on the businesses that enter, or attempt to enter, the new legal market. This creates very real and expensive compliance risks for legal entrants. Business owners and investors are rightly scared by the many possible ways of unintentionally violating some rule, or of encountering a particularly aggressive and perhaps mistaken state or local inspector, and getting into expensive trouble—or, worse, having the business shut down.

Higher-than-usual costs of capital and expected profits for investors, along with higher wages and other costs on the supply side (compared with profits or costs of less risky businesses), are examples of "risk premiums" showing up in the legal weed market, just as risk premiums have traditionally been observed in the illegal weed market. For instance, average interest rates for debt financing and average rents per square foot in the legal weed industry have been observed to be higher than the average for other industries, reflecting risk premiums for landlords as well. Higher income or margin expectations in the case that the project succeeds may compensate legal weed investors or entrepreneurs for their greater perceived chances of losing their investment (as many have done) compared with investing their money or time in other nonweed business opportunities.

So you have not just an illegal risk premium but also a legal risk premium. In a few places with modest demands on license holders and clear, transparent rules, the legal risk premium may be low and declining as businesses and enforcers both learn the rules. But in other places with particularly challenging barriers to legal entry or particularly stiff enforcement of sanctions against licensed rule breakers, legal risk premiums could become, or may already be, bigger than illegal risk premiums. Legal risk premiums might make weed even more expensive in those markets, on top of all the other state and local compliance costs and (as we will now discuss) taxes that are unique to the legal market—adding one more star to the constellation of economic challenges faced by legal weed.

One of the many big risks of legal weed is the risk of not paying taxes correctly, including not only all the normal business taxes on payrolls, other inputs, and retail sales, but also cannabis taxes, which are high and complicated in most places in North America.

Taxes on Legal Weed

For legal weed, the price paid by the consumer typically includes some general sales or value-added taxes and some cannabis-specific taxes. Taxes that vary by state and local jurisdiction are added at the point of sale, so they are visible to the consumer. Other taxes may be applied earlier in the supply chain. Some taxes are additive, and some, like sales taxes, are figured as a percentage of the price, which may already include other taxes and markups.

In California, a cultivation tax of $9.65 per ounce ($154.40 per pound) of flower is assessed when the product leaves the farm stage. At the wholesale stage, a state excise tax of about 27 percent of wholesale price is assessed (the state assumes this is equivalent to about 15 percent of retail price, with a 1.8 ratio of retail price to wholesale price). Some California retail prices quoted on the menus of weed shops or delivery services include the state excise tax, while other prices do not include the excise tax and instead add it to the price at the point of purchase. Few price listings include local sales tax (which averages 8.3 percent statewide) or local cannabis taxes (0–15 percent) that are added on top of the cultivation tax and state excise tax.

Depending on how you compound these numbers and what part of California you're in, the net effect is equivalent to a tax rate of around 35 to 50 percent of the retail price for legal weed, which already starts out quite a bit higher than the illegal weed price because of all the regulatory costs along the supply chain. Table 1 shows a simple calculation of how California's various stages of taxation affect the end price paid by consumers for legal weed in one of the state's several jurisdictions where the local retail weed tax is 10 percent.

TABLE 1. Example of effects of taxation on legal ⅛-ounce flower in California

Stage	Untaxed	Taxed	
Farm price	$12.00	$12.00	Starting farm price per eighth
		$13.21	After $154.40/lb cultivation tax
Wholesale price	$23.72	$24.93	After $1,500/lb wholesale markup
		$31.65	After 27% excise tax
Retail price	$43.25	$51.19	After $2,500/lb retail markup
		$56.30	After 10% local tax
		$60.55	After 8.3% sales tax
End price	**$43.25**	**$60.55**	Price paid by consumers
		$17.30	Difference between taxed and untaxed price
		40.0%	**Implied net compound tax rate**

Note: Assumes a farm price of about $1,536 per pound or $12.00 per eighth, which our data from Cannabis Benchmarks suggest was typical for legal weed in California as of mid-2021.

We calculate the effects of taxes by measuring the difference between two scenarios: an "untaxed" scenario, where no taxes are imposed at any stage, and a "taxed" scenario, where all the taxes are applied.

You will notice that the results in Table 1 depend on our assumed middleman "markups" between farm and wholesale (the "wholesale markup") and between wholesale and retail (the "retail markup"). Estimating these markups is a tricky business. Different industries and companies handle price markups from one stage to the next differently. One rule of thumb in many industries is that markups from one stage to the next are on a percentage basis. But why would it make more sense for wholesale and retail markups to be percentages (e.g., an "80 percent markup," or 1.8x multiple of the cost of goods), rather than a fixed dollar fee to reflect the dollar cost or value added at each stage?

In real-world businesses, most markups are some hybrid of percentage and additive—reflecting the fact that some costs incurred by wholesalers and retailers (e.g., transport, business administration) are probably similar for lower-priced and higher-priced products, while other costs (e.g., packaging, marketing) are probably more expensive for the higher-priced products. In our simple calculations in Table 1, which correspond roughly to some real-life data we've looked at in California, we assume that wholesalers impose a (flat-dollar-amount) markup of $1,500 per pound and that retailers impose a markup of $2,500 per pound.

One thing to notice about the tax effect calculations shown in Table 1 is that taxes at different stages have different effects. In our example, the price of $12.00 per eighth ($1,536 per pound) is the untaxed "farm price." The initial cultivation tax paid on that eighth by the farmer is $1.21. But the net effect of the cultivation tax on the consumer is more than $1.21, because other taxes are applied on top of amounts that include the cultivation tax. The net cost of the cultivation tax to the consumer (as measured by the difference between the taxed and untaxed scenarios if you remove the cultivation tax) is actually $1.81 per eighth.

If, instead of assuming fixed-dollar-amount markups as we do in Table 1, you assume 80 percent markups at each of the two stages (wholesale and retail), then you end up with a much bigger estimate of the net cost of the cultivation tax to the consumer: $5.88 per eighth—almost five times the $1.21 cultivation tax imposed at the farm.

So one lesson we learned from doing this exercise ourselves is that however you measure markups, seemingly moderate cannabis cultivation taxes end up being expensive to consumers per dollar of government revenue raised (compared with retail taxes, for instance) because as early-stage taxes ripple downstream toward the consumer, they are multiplied along the way by markups.

How Can Legal Weed Compete?

In much of North America, with taxes, regulatory costs, and other impediments that we discussed earlier, legal weed after tax can often cost twice as much as illegal weed.

Let's say, as a hypothetical example, that the legal weed in your state costs $45 after tax and the illegal weed costs $25.

The $45 package of legal weed probably has nicer packaging and branding than the $25 package of illegal weed. And why not? All of the other costs are so big that they make spending an extra couple dollars on fancy packaging, which will deliver extra perceived value to some consumers, look like a no-brainer for the legal weed seller.

How else might the consumer consider the legal weed a fair value, given the fundamental indistinguishability of the contents of the package? Maybe, for a few weed buyers, the safety testing has lots of value, but for most probably not.

On the other hand, the illegal weed producers have been stepping it up with the packaging too and have even created counterfeit and knock-off legal weed packages with fake testing certifications. Such innovations in illegal weed marketing can make illegal weed an even closer substitute for legal weed.

The consumer might pay a little more for the illegal weed in legal-looking packaging than for the illegal weed in a plastic baggie, but either way, the illegal weed is usually sold at a very good

The $40 Standard—Old and New

For decades, across the North American illegal market, from the Atlantic to the Pacific, weed prices were discussed in terms of the most typical form of weed: an eighth, or ⅛ ounce of flower. An eighth is the standard package that people have been buying from illegal street dealers and delivery services for decades, long before any form of legalization was passed anywhere in North America. The vast majority of illegal weed in recent history has been sold as eighths of flower.

Although the North American legal weed markets have far more product variety than any illegal weed market has ever had anywhere, an eighth of flower, according to our data, is also still by far the most popular legal weed package in the United States. Legal or illegal, the eighth is king. That's why we like it as an example and use it often throughout this book as a benchmark when we discuss prices.

As of around 1990, before any form of legalization arrived, across most of the U.S. an eighth of illegal weed would typically cost about $40. It would be nearly impossible to establish this with a random sample of hard data: it is an anecdotal observation collected from interviews with people who have had intimate experience with the illegal market over the last half century. (Ask your friends and neighbors who were around 30 or 40 years ago and see if their memories match those of people we talked to.) Prices seem to have varied by state, but not as much as they do now in the legal weed market (as we will show you later in the chapter). In 1990, the price of an eighth of illegal weed might have been $30 in California or Washington, and $50 in New York or Massachusetts. But by most accounts, the modal price around the United States was $40.

Interestingly, as of 2021, the median and mean prices for legal retail weed in many U.S. states are still not far from $40 per eighth. But beneath this seeming consistency lies a world of price variation between different kinds of weed and between different states.

If $40 per eighth has been a "sticky" price range for weed through the years, it would be totally wrong to say that the typical real price of weed in general hasn't changed since the days when all of it was illegal. First, don't forget inflation. The dollar cost of goods and services now is twice as high as it was 30 years ago. This means that $40 today buys about half as much as it did in 1990—except you get the same eighth of weed. Second, actually it is not the *same* eighth. Weed potency has gone up, and gone up a lot. By all accounts, most legal weed is several times more potent than illegal weed was back in the day. However, today's illegal weed has caught up with legal weed and is often equally potent.

Interestingly, if the value of a dollar fell by half over the same period that weed potency doubled, then you could say that the real price of weed had fallen by a factor of four. But, alas, we know of no reliable data on weed potency over time.

price compared with legal weed and represents a good value proposition for most buyers.

Legalization Changed Retail Weed

Legalization has changed the nature of weed prices in several fundamental ways. Two of the big effects we see in the legal market are:

Effect 1. Product Diversification. Most of our story has been about weed flower. But, as we hope is clear by now, not all weed is flower: far from it. The first big change brought by legalization has been a huge variety of different product types and package sizes. Talking about "the price of weed" in today's legal market means talking not only about the price of flower but also about the prices of vape pens and cartridges, wax, shatter, tincture, and many other forms of weed that are now commonly available at virtually every legal retail store, including food products much more varied than the traditional brownies and cookies.

The recreational markets have brought a rapid and extensive diversification of weed products. Back in the fully illegal days, in the 1990s, the large majority of mostly one product—smokable flower—was sold to end consumers either by the eighth of an ounce ("eighth") or by the ounce, although smaller packages (such as $10 "dime bags") could also be found. (Back in the 1960s and 1970s, illegal consumers more frequently bought by the ounce or even sometimes by the pound, at much lower prices.) Most consumers smoked the flower either in a joint (or "spliff," mixed with tobacco) or from a pipe (glass, metal, wood, or plastic) or a "bong" (water pipe).

In the old days some consumers made their own home-baked goods, but few used electric "vaporizers" that applied heat to the flower and created inhalable vapor without smoke. A few decades ago, the few vaporizers around were mostly tabletop devices that plugged into a wall outlet.

Alongside the legal weed market, a new technology entered: pocket-sized battery-powered vaporizers, a.k.a. "vape pens," which vaporize concentrated cannabis oil (typically between 60 and 90 percent THC) that is encapsulated in plastic or glass. The product is more compact than flower, is not consumed by bringing smoke into the lungs, and is less smelly—an advantage for traveling in places where weed is illegal. Some vape pens are disposable, while others use replaceable oil cartridges. Vape pens have boomed in the past decade and in some states have taken 30 percent or more of the retail consumer weed market by value. Gummies are another product whose sales are growing fast.

As measured by cost per unit of THC (the most common measure of weed potency), buying a vape pen is a much more expensive way of consuming weed than simply buying smokable flower and rolling paper. A typical eighth of flower (⅛ ounce = 3.54 grams) might cost $40 and have 20 percent THC by volume, which works out to a price of about $56 per gram (before tax) for 0.7 grams of pure THC. On the other hand, if you spend your money on a vape pen or cartridge, you might pay twice as much per gram of pure THC. This reflects, in part, the producer's additional cost of distilling the flower into oil and manufacturing the device.

Effect 2. Premiumization. Another major difference between the new world of legal weed and the old world of illegal weed is premiumization. In the old world, many illegal dealers would have just one type of weed for sale, at a single price point, typically discounted at higher quantities (for instance: $40 per eighth, $250 per ounce). The most sophisticated dealers in the prelegalization world sometimes offered two or three different quality levels of weed at slightly differentiated price points. For instance, high-grade "kind bud" (generally indoor-grown and higher-potency) might have been priced at $50 per eighth, midgrade (generally outdoor-grown) at $40 per eighth, and low-grade "schwag" (with smaller buds and more stems and seeds) at $25 or $30 per eighth. But the range was not nearly as wide as today. In those days, the weed price spread was like the spread among standard supermarket carrots.

Today's legal weed retailers, and the illegal weed suppliers who compete with them, make even the most differentiated corners of the old illegal world look quaint. The contemporary legal weed dispensary is more like a gourmet food shop, with a blossoming of different product types and quality levels at the premium end of the price spectrum. Even in standard supermarkets these days you can buy white, brown, large, small, organic, cage-free, free-range, and maybe pasture-raised eggs at prices ranging from $1 per dozen to more than $1 per egg. Similarly, you can now buy weed at prices ranging from $3 to more than $100 per gram of pure THC equivalent. Weed has started to look like the modern-day beer market, where products range from the cheapest commercial brands to the fancy local craft beers. The price spread between the top and bottom of beer prices is 30 to 1, versus the 12-to-1 price spread for eggs. (Neither is anywhere close to the mind-boggling 1,000-to-1 price spread of wine retail, where a new bottle could cost anywhere from $2 to $2,000.)

Snoop, Seth Rogen, Mike Tyson, Jay-Z, Bob Marley's estate, and many more have launched their own premium weed brands. Legal weed brands might be marketed on their region of origin (Figure 9), their organic farming methods (Figure 10), or their craft auteurs (Figure 11). There are weed brands targeting increasingly niche markets, from paleo and gluten-free consumers (Figure 12), to seniors, to Gen-X-ers nostalgic for the 1960s or the 1980s (Figure 13).

One of the most expensive weed products on the North American legal market, in terms of price per gram of pure THC, is the Dosist (Figure 14), a special type of vape pen that automatically dispenses premeasured 2.5-milligram puffs, with several different models claiming to have different effects such as "bliss," "arouse," and "calm." Dosist was first introduced to the market in 2016 at a retail price of about $40 for a 112.5-milligram pen with 82 percent

FIGURES 9–13. Credit: Robin Goldstein.

FIGURE 14. "Dosist" vape pens with their claimed effects. Credit: Robin Goldstein.

THC cannabis oil—a heroic $433 per gram of pure THC, or almost $39,000 per pound of 20 percent THC flower equivalent. (Dosist prices have since come down somewhat.)

Even with the portable vape boom, tabletop vaporizers haven't disappeared: on the contrary, the tabletop market has continued to

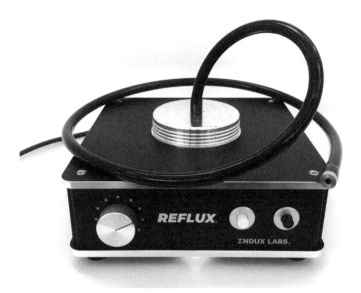

FIGURE 15. Reflux vaporizer from Indux Labs, retail price $1,710. Credit: Indux Labs.

premiumize in the age of legal weed. In past decades, a device called the Volcano, with a distinctive inflatable-balloon design, was famously the most expensive vaporizer on the market, at $500 or $600 for top-of-the-line models.

No longer: nowadays it's possible to spend up to $3,000 for a home vaporizer. A company called Indux Labs makes a tabletop model called the Reflux (list price $1,710, shown in Figure 15) and a battery-powered briefcase vaporizer called 7Ten (list price $2,999), reinforcing the age-old adage that there is no upper limit to how much consumers are willing to pay for a product, especially if those consumers (and their incomes) are high enough.

Weed, Tobacco, and Alcohol

Throughout this book, we periodically draw comparisons between weed and two markets that have much in common with weed, especially in terms of heavy government regulation: tobacco and alcohol. As far as we can tell, as of the fall of 2021, every legal weed market in North America prohibits weed retailers from also selling tobacco or alcohol. Weed retailers can sell nonweed products (e.g., weed pipes, accessories, lighters, tie-dyed T-shirts, or hemp-cloth tote bags), but they can't be bars, restaurants serving alcohol, or retail alcohol or tobacco stores.

In North America, one of the most popular ways to consume weed is to smoke a blunt: a hollowed-out cigar refilled with weed. Blunts have long been big in the hip-hop crowd, piggybacking off the popularity of cigars. Also popular is the spliff: a hand-rolled joint that combines tobacco with weed. Spliffs first came of age in the Netherlands, where they're still one of the most common ways that people in Amsterdam smoke their (legal) weed. The Dutch like everything in moderation, and by cutting the weed with tobacco, a spliff provides a milder high than a pure weed joint. In recent years, spliff culture has also spread across North America, joining the long-standing blunt culture.

However, as far as we know, not a single U.S. state or Canadian province allows for legal weed-tobacco hybrids such as blunts or spliffs. Prerolled joints must be 100 percent weed (or, occasionally, weed with an herbal mix that doesn't contain tobacco). So blunts and spliffs, which in some circles are far more popular than pure weed joints, cannot be sold legally. This limits the market for pre-rolls, which, unregulated, would likely include pre-rolled blunts and spliffs.

Why the prohibition on alcohol sales together with weed sales? First, some background. "On-premise sale" is alcohol-industry lingo for the sale of alcohol for consumption at the place where the alcohol is sold—for example in a bar, restaurant, or café—which must hold an "on-premise" beer, wine, or liquor license. "Off-premise sale," on the other hand, means the sale of alcohol for taking away and drinking at home (or anywhere else other than the place where the alcohol is sold). In the United States, as of 2018, about 56 percent of alcohol sales, by retail value (in dollars), was on-premise sales, and 44 percent was off-premise sales. By quantity (in gallons of alcohol), the proportions would reverse, because prices are much higher per gallon in on-premise sales. (These numbers changed in 2020–21 when COVID-19-related regulations shut down large portions of the on-premise industry.)

The cannabis equivalent to the bar or restaurant—a place for on-premise cannabis consumption—has traditionally been known as a "coffeeshop." This genre was pioneered in the Netherlands, where the sale and consumption of weed have been partially decriminalized for 50 years. Amsterdam's first coffeeshop, Mellow Yellow, opened in 1972. Over the decades that followed, more than 200 coffeeshops opened in Amsterdam, and the coffeeshops became a major tourist draw.

From the beginning, most Dutch coffeeshops not only sold weed but also provided rooms with tables and chairs where you could smoke it on the spot. On-premise weed consumption has always been an integral part of the Dutch coffeeshop experience. Coffeeshop customers value the novelty not only of buying legal weed (which, for decades, was a unique phenomenon in the world) but also of being able to sit down and enjoy it with friends and strangers in a social environment.

In recent years, government measures aimed at reducing drug tourism and crime have limited the location and number of coffeeshops, including proposed restriction of sales to Dutch residents only. But whatever happens in the future, Dutch coffeeshops will always have an important place in the global history of legal weed.

Back in North America, some states with legal weed have set up systems where on-premise consumption is not prohibited under state law, thus allowing for the possibility of Dutch-style coffeeshops, or (as they have been more commonly called in the United States) "cannabis cafés," "smoking lounges," "vape lounges," or "social consumption lounges." In keeping with the lingo of our book, we'll call them "weed lounges."

In January 2018, California became the first U.S. state to open the door for legal on-premise cannabis consumption—not by explicitly authorizing it under state law but simply by not prohibiting it, thus giving local governments the option of allowing it. Local governments in a few California municipalities, including San Francisco and West Hollywood, subsequently authorized a few weed lounges.

The first to open, in early 2018, was Barbary Coast in downtown San Francisco. A handful of other weed lounges have since opened in the Bay Area, as well as in Colorado, where state law now provides an opening for on-premise consumption, again subject to local approval, which has been granted to some establishments in Denver (as reported in *High Times* in April 2021). However, from the early evidence in California, even before COVID-19-related restrictions suspended a lot of on-premise activity, the genre does not seem to have caught on. Barbary Coast seems to have done okay, but customers weren't showing up in droves. Of the local

The Professional Bicycle Fisherman

By Robin

Amsterdam is a weird place.

One day in 2002, I was visiting the city with some friends. We had just left a coffeeshop along a canal where some Jamaicans were selling legal weed to some Romanians. That was pretty weird, especially 20 years ago, when people in most U.S. states were still being locked up for first-time possession of weed. But maybe even weirder, my friends and I were headed to a third-floor pancake house that could be entered only by climbing a narrow ladder and ducking into a two-thirds-height doorway. The place was a hot spot for all the local folks who had the same edition of Lonely Planet as we had.

On our way to the pancake house, we turned down what we thought would be an uncrowded back canal to find three-deep rows of tourists along the sidewalk. Hundreds of people were craning their necks to see something in the canal. This was before cell-phone photos existed, so these poor people were trying to see things with their own eyes. As tourists, my friends and I had an immediate and involuntary desire to look at whatever a large number of other tourists were looking at. We hatched a plan and staked out a view from a bridge over the secondary canal around the corner.

The sight we finally saw was a long, slow-moving trawler, gliding along the still water at an almost imperceptibly slow speed. It was staffed by a fat, sunburnt older man, dressed from head to toe in municipal orange. The man was sitting on top of the trawler. We soon realized that this was no ordinary man: he was a bicycle fisherman employed by the city of Amsterdam. He might have been one of the only professional bicycle fishermen in the world.

The professional bicycle fisherman looked calm, almost sleepy, as he reclined in a spinning chair in the winter sun, his hand on the classic joystick of heavy machinery, lowering the forklift into the water and retrieving some of the hundreds of bicycles that sat at the bottom of the city's many shallow canals.

Every dip of the giant iron jaws, expertly guided by the professional bicycle fisherman into the mess of olive goo that flowed beneath Amsterdam's gently arching bridges, would yield four or five partially crushed bikes. The jaws would toss them into the heap of others, like a time-lapse junkyard growing over four seasons in the middle of a long boat.

Any city of canals must deal with certain brutal fiscal realities. I am not sure if Venice or Huangzhou has a municipal bicycle-fishing budget. But on the day I saw Amsterdam's professional bicycle fisherman, I realized that some problems could also arise from legal weed.

on-premise authorizations granted, only a small minority have actually opened.

Why not? Why haven't weed lounges taken off in San Francisco and Los Angeles? Figure 16 might offer a clue.

We think an important factor holding back on-premise weed may be the state prohibition on consuming alcohol and weed on the same premises. Here's the problem: Pick a typical group of friends who like to socialize, and you will often find a mix of what people like to consume. Some prefer to have a beer, a glass of wine, or a cocktail. Others prefer to smoke some weed instead. And others (perhaps even the majority of weed smokers) prefer to do both: drink and smoke during the same social occasion. Many North American weed consumers, however much they like their weed, still think of alcohol as their go-to social drug of choice, and would sooner forgo weed than forgo alcohol when they go out. And for some consumers, weed is not their social drug but rather their drug for more intimate settings.

Of course, in many states where weed is legal, forgoing weed isn't even necessary at a bar: although California and some other

FIGURE 16. The strict state-mandated prohibition on alcohol and tobacco consumption at Barbary Coast in San Francisco, California's first on-premise weed-smoking lounge. Credit: Robin Goldstein.

states technically have restrictions on smoking weed in public, the restrictions do not appear to be enforced anywhere in the state. So people who go to a bar often pop out onto the sidewalk to smoke their weed (or tobacco) and come back in for their drinks. Or they can vape in the bathroom, or chew on edibles beforehand. In short, it's pretty easy to consume weed with alcohol in a social setting at a bar.

On the other hand, it's illegal and difficult to bring alcohol into a weed lounge, and it's illegal (in the vast majority of North America) to hold an open container of alcohol on a sidewalk. And unlike the unenforced outdoor-weed-smoking laws, open-container laws are sometimes enforced against consumers, whether by weed-lounge security or by local police.

Simple calculation of costs and benefits suggests that a group of friends with a diverse mix of weed-versus-alcohol preferences will be likely to choose an ordinary bar, where they can consume everything they want to consume, over a weed lounge, where they can consume only some of what they want to consume. Plus, many states have curfews for legal weed sales at midnight or even 10 p.m., limiting the possibilities for late-night revelry (more on this in the next section). So we think that until state and local laws allow both on-premise weed and alcohol consumption at the same establishments (if they ever do) and lift hours-of-operation restrictions, the North American market for on-premise weed consumption (Figure 16) is likely to remain small.

Another element of the on-premise alcohol market is outdoor parties and festivals. Here, too, in California, on-premise weed consumption runs into the same problem. With California's 2018 recreational legalization, the state also created a "Cannabis Event Organizer License," where weed can be smoked openly in a gated-off area. But this type of license also prohibits drinking and smoking weed in the same area.

In California, the Cannabis Event Organizer License has mostly been a bust. Relatively few businesses applied for licenses, and the few events that have been held, by most accounts, weren't very well attended. Again, we think the alcohol prohibition is probably a major reason for the lack of interest. For many consumers, whether or not you're allowed to get stoned, a festival where you can't drink with your friends isn't really much of a festival.

Late-Night Weed

Speaking of festivals, the late-night party hours of 10 p.m. to 2 a.m. are a prime time to buy weed, just as they are a prime time to buy beer. In Las Vegas, the late-night city supreme, several legal weed retailers are open 24 hours and buzz throughout the night. In Colorado and Washington, on the other hand, weed can't be sold legally after midnight, so all weed sales after midnight move completely to the illegal market.

In California and Arizona, the curfew for legal weed retailing is even earlier: 10 p.m. To many California weed retailers, this news came as a shock. Before 2018, when California implemented its new legal recreational system, there were no statewide restrictions on hours of operation for medical weed retail. Starting on January 1, 2018, all legal weed retail (recreational or medical) became illegal after 10 p.m.

Table 2 first looks at the situation in 2017 and shows that 63 percent of medical retailers were open after 10 p.m., and 26 percent of medical retailers were open after midnight.

By our rough estimates, when the 10 p.m. curfew went into effect on January 1, 2018, about 13 percent of the state's total opening hours for legal weed were eliminated. These calculations are shown in the bottom half of Table 2, where we estimate the number of lost opening hours per day in six California cities.

Under California's new version of "legalization," people must now turn to illegal dealers (mostly delivery services) to buy their weed during prime party hours. All night long, you can buy weed

TABLE 2. Effects of California's hours-of-operation restrictions on previously operating medical dispensaries

	Hours of medical retailers operating in 2017			
City	Obs.	Avg closing time	% open after 10 p.m.	% open after midnight
Los Angeles	24	12:20 a.m.	83%	33%
San Francisco	18	10:53 p.m.	50%	17%
San Diego	16	11:56 p.m.	75%	38%
San Jose	10	11:50 p.m.	30%	20%
Sacramento	8	11:08 p.m.	63%	13%
Davis	6	10:40 p.m.	50%	17%
Statewide averages	**82**	**11:51 p.m.**	**63%**	**26%**

	Business hours that would be illegalized by a 10 p.m. curfew					
	Avg effect on impacted businesses			Effect averaged across all businesses statewide (including late-night businesses and non-late-night businesses)		
City	Lost hrs/ day	Lost hrs/yr	% of total hrs*	Lost hrs/ day	Lost hrs/yr	% of total hrs*
Los Angeles	2.90	1,015	21%	2.42	846	17%
San Francisco	2.33	817	19%	1.17	408	9%
San Diego	2.75	963	20%	2.06	722	15%
San Jose	4.00	1,400	33%	1.20	20	10%
Sacramento	2.40	840	19%	1.50	525	12%
Davis	1.67	583	14%	0.83	292	7%
Statewide averages	**2.71**	**949**	**20%**	**1.72**	**602**	**13%**

*Assumes uniform statewide average opening time of 10:30 a.m.

only from a criminal. It is hard to imagine that this turn of events had a positive effect on public safety in East L.A., or anywhere else in California.

Can Legal Weed Win?

Let's come back to the kickoff questions with which we started this chapter and this book. Weed is expensive first because of high costs of production and marketing, starting on the farm. Only small marketable quantities—measured in pounds rather than tons—come from each acre, worker, or million dollars of capital. It turns out that for many suppliers, the costs of being legal are even higher than the costs of remaining in the illegal market. Legal weed businesses face costly regulations and taxes at every stage of the supply chain. It also turns out that many of the biggest weed customers do not value buying from the legal weed emporium all that much more than buying from their traditional guy. Indeed, as we have noted, for some weed buyers it is less hassle to buy illegal weed.

Clearly, the high costs of being legal, compared to the lower costs of being illegal, limit the current opportunity for legal weed to grow its share. But another factor in the economic calculation is the set of rules that place a drag on legal consumption at any price, such as local restrictions on where legal retailers can locate and statewide restrictions on the hours when legal weed retailers can operate. Since legal weed retailers are not allowed to make sales where and when their competitors can, they are limited in their ability to attract customers.

Every regulation has some rationale behind it. But there are some regulations, like California's 10 p.m. curfew—which means that legal weed loses all of its late-night share to illegal drug dealers and alcohol—where it is very hard to see a convincing public safety rationale for a statewide ban. Instead, in situations where legal transactions are prohibited, retail weed is pushed into the hands of illegal dealers. Consumer and public safety almost surely suffer. To many observers of the early years of legal weed in America, it is not clear that the public benefits of the extensive restrictions justify the damage they have done to legal weed businesses across North America.

4 *We Ask Our Data*

Where's the Cheapest Legal Weed?

Until now, we have spoken only in rough terms about the price of weed. We now turn to some interesting patterns we see in data we have been working with for the past six years.

In this chapter, we draw on a large data set of U.S. online retail weed prices that we have been collecting in our research group at UC Davis since 2016. We also draw on data from Cannabis Benchmarks, which collects wholesale farm prices for weed in several U.S. states.

The retail prices we collect are listed by U.S. weed retailers on Weedmaps, an online retail listing and e-commerce website. Weedmaps was founded in 2008 and has long been the leading weed retail portal in America. Many in the industry consider a listing on Weedmaps to be an essential cost of doing business for a legal retailer. In California, for instance, about 70 percent of state-licensed weed retailers have a Weedmaps listing—and not all licensed retailers are open for business, so an even higher percentage of open retailers maintain a presence on Weedmaps. Weedmaps charges listing fees to retailers ranging from several hundred dollars per year to several thousand dollars per month.

Across the U.S., there are about 7,600 unique Weedmaps retailers with listings in 38 states (including the territory of Puerto Rico, which for simplicity we hereafter include when we say "states"). Weedmaps also have lots of Canadian listings, but we do not present Canadian data in this chapter.

Each retailer lists prices for different types of weed and weed products, including standard flower packages, oil cartridges, and other products. The retailer product lists include listing by brand and product characteristics. Retailers vary in their listing practices. Some retailers list only a few prices, some list dozens or hundreds, and some list thousands. Most Weedmaps prices do not include state and local cannabis and sales taxes that are imposed at retail. So such retail prices do not reflect the total end price paid by the consumer. Cultivation taxes are included, because those taxes are paid before the product ends up on the retail shelf.

Some details about our retail price data set are important. Where there is most difference in interpretation across retailers is over state excise taxes: some retailers appear to include excise taxes in their posted prices, while others do not. Also, we cannot tell how representative the Weedmaps samples are of all licensed establishments, because there's no comprehensive database of prices from all licensed establishments. Almost all legal weed retailers have websites or online listings of some kind, but there are different formats that seem to be more or less common in different places.

Although (like any "big data" set) our data set has some drawbacks, the general trends we observe, and the comparisons we make between regions, seem to be the best available and are useful to get a window on the industry. We collect, filter, and clean millions of observations in each time period that we sample. We think Weedmaps has the largest data set in the world of retail cannabis prices that can be analyzed in a standardized format that allows for statistical comparisons. We leap into these data to see what patterns emerge.

One more clarification: in some states (especially California), some delivery-only retail operations list themselves dozens of times on Weedmaps with one identical listing for each distinct town or neighborhood within their delivery radius. This does not mean that they are running multiple delivery services; rather, it is simply an advertising or marketing strategy to blanket a large regional area by posting many listings for the same delivery service that seems very "local" in many specific nearby places. In our data-cleaning process, we take steps to avoid counting such listings multiple times. When we find a delivery-only retailer with multiple listings showing identical business names, license numbers, phone numbers, menu items, and prices, we count the retailer and its prices only once, and we exclude the duplicate listings. This de-duplication process reduced the size of our data set from about 11,000 retailers to about 7,600 *unique* retailers in the 38 U.S. states (including Puerto Rico), with the vast majority of removed duplicates coming from California. De-duplication reduced the number of price observations in the data set from 4.2 million to 2.6 million.

In our analysis for this book, we used an October 2021 online snapshot from Weedmaps. We excluded states with fewer than 20 retailers, because we had less confidence that those samples were representative of their states. This narrowed the number of states in the data used for analysis from 38 states to 22 states but excluded only about 1 percent of total retailers and 0.3 percent of total prices. The remaining data we spend the rest of the chapter reviewing have about 7,500 weed retailers in 22 states that listed about 2.5 million distinct cannabis products with associated prices. Table 3 gives

TABLE 3. Retailer prevalence and sample size by state in our cannabis retail price data set
*Twenty two U.S. states with Weedmaps data, ordered by retailers per capita listing on Weedmaps.
Price observations include only common package sizes of flower and oil. Excludes states with
fewer than 20 retailers listed.*

State	State population per Weedmaps retailer	Total Weedmaps retailers	Total price observations
Oklahoma	3,060	1,294	468,250
Maine	3,926	347	63,760
Montana	4,797	226	2,930
Oregon	6,222	681	216,207
Alaska	6,490	113	27,397
Colorado	7,450	775	159,558
Washington	17,433	442	269,987
New Mexico	17,646	120	4,269
Michigan	17,995	560	289,017
Puerto Rico	23,140	142	21,504
California	24,168	1,636	806,457
Nevada	30,739	101	50,131
Massachusetts	38,415	183	24,447
Arizona	62,187	115	34,088
Maryland	63,033	98	35,738
Missouri	66,182	93	11,418
Arkansas	83,653	36	9,188
Florida	97,901	220	5,991
Pennsylvania	122,667	106	1,539
Illinois	152,530	84	33,821
Ohio	203,439	58	8,303
New York	492,713	41	2,347
Recreational states (11)	**19,759**	**5,037**	**1,974,870**
Medical-only states[a] (11)	**37,934**	**2,434**	**571,477**
All states (22)	**25,680**	**7,471**	**2,546,347**

Sources: Retailers from Weedmaps (October 2021); state populations from U.S. Census
Bureau.

[a] Includes the territory of Puerto Rico.

Shaded states = Legal recreational sales were in place as of 2021. (Montana, New Mexico, and New York had passed legalization laws but had not yet opened legal recreational sales, so all open legal weed retailers were medical in those states.)

an overview of this retail price data set, ordered by the per capita prevalence of retailers in each state.

The main purpose of Table 3 is simply to paint a broad picture of the data we will use to observe patterns about retail weed prices in the rest of the chapter. First, some explanations: when we say "Total Weedmaps retailers" (the middle numerical column in Table 3), we mean the total of retailer pages listed on Weedmaps with a unique name and menu of prices.

In Table 3 the numbers in the leftmost numerical column are simply the state population divided by the number of retailers in the state, which yields the number of people per retailer. Lower numbers represent more retailer-dense states. Density varies widely by state, from about one Weedmaps retailer per 3,000 people in the very retailer-dense state of Oklahoma to about one retailer per 500,000 people in the very retailer-sparse state of New York. In the 22 states combined, there is an average of about one Weedmaps retailer per 26,000 people.

Recreational States Have More Retailers

One clear pattern emerges from Table 3 when we compare states with recreational legalization (of which there are 11 in the Weedmaps data set, shaded in gray in Table 3) with states that still have medical-only legalization (of which there are also 11). Overall, our data suggest that states with recreational legalization tend to have more listings per capita on Weedmaps. The 11 recreational states have an aggregate population of about 100 million and have a total of about 5,000 Weedmaps retailers (about 20,000 people per retailer). The 11 medical-only states have an aggregate population of about 92 million and have a total of about 2,400 retailers (about 38,000 people per retailer). We also note that recreational states have generally been offering legal weed for longer than the medical-only states.

On the top end of retailers per capita, 7 of the 11 most retailer-dense states (with more than one retailer per 25,000 people) are states with recreational legalization. On the other end of the spectrum, 7 of the 9 most retailer-sparse states (with less than one retailer per 60,000 people) are medical-only states. So a clear pattern emerges connecting recreational legalization to retailer density on Weedmaps.

Two notable exceptions to the recreational-medical density pattern are the medical-only states of Oklahoma (#1 in retailer density overall, with one retailer per 3,060 people) and Montana (#3, with one retailer per 4,797 people). Like Maine (#2) and Alaska (#5), Montana is a rural, sparsely populated state where proportionally more stores or delivery services are needed to serve a given number of households, since the households are spaced so far apart. But rural effects don't do much to explain the formidable weed retail density of Oklahoma, which is in the middle of the U.S. states in population density and share of rural population. Oklahoma, with four million people, has more total retail listings on Weedmaps (1,294) than any U.S. state other than California (which has 10 times the population!). It is also worth noting that Oklahoma leads in price observations per capita, which means its many retailers are well stocked with distinct products. The Oklahoma miracle doesn't end with retail store or product density; we'll come back to Oklahoma's unique legal weed achievements later in the chapter.

Normal Weed Often Costs $40 per Eighth

We next move on to weed retail prices. Our 2.5 million U.S. price observations from 22 states include different quantity sizes of the same basic item (e.g., ⅛ ounce vs. ¼ ounce of the same brand and strain of flower).

If we had to report only one result from this large Weedmaps data set, it would be this: the retail price of legal weed in the United States is about $40 per eighth. The most common weed package, ⅛ ounce of flower, or an "eighth," has a median listed price of $40 and a mean price of $40.32, based on about 240,000 price observations. See Chapter 3 for more on the $40 standard price for weed.

But weed prices are not just flower prices. Cannabis oil, mostly in the form of cartridges and vape pens, makes up more than one-third of the retail market by value in some states, so we also look at retail oil prices. The most common oil package size (in terms of total number of retail price listings) is 1 gram. The median U.S. listed price for 1 gram of cannabis oil on Weedmaps is $42, and the mean price is $43.94, based on about 190,000 price observations.

Our data enable us to compare prices within two important weed categories: psychoactive cannabis oil and psychoactive cannabis flower. But are they comparable products? How does the amount of weed in an eighth of flower compare with the amount of weed in a gram of oil?

Short answer: they're about the same. Longer answer: THC is thought to be the most psychoactive ingredient in weed, and weed's potency is often measured by THC content. A typical 1-gram oil cartridge (or vape pen) with 70 percent THC contains almost exactly the same amount of pure THC equivalent (about 0.7 grams) as a typical ⅛-ounce package of flower with 20 percent THC. That means the ⅛-ounce flower and 1-gram oil packages make for a straightforward comparison of prices for different forms of weed with the same amount of "active ingredient."

The data show that you're paying about 5 percent more ($42 versus $40) to get your eighth of weed in oil form rather than flower form. This oil price premium of about 5 percent above the ⅛-ounce flower price, for roughly the same 0.7 grams of THC, could be reasonably explained, on the supply side, by the additional processing and material costs of pressing oil and packaging it into metal, glass, and/or plastic cartridges. On the demand side it means that some buyers are willing to pay to buy the delivery system offered by a cartridge rather than smoking the weed flower directly.

The fact that the U.S. median and mean prices are close to each other, both for ⅛ ounce of flower and 1 gram of oil—and not just for the country as a whole, but for individual states as well—suggests that the price data may have something close to a normal distribution (i.e., with a mass centered on the mean and similar-looking tails above and below the mean). Consistent with this mean-median agreement, we observe the same broad trends in the data whether we choose means or medians as representations of price in a given state or time period. Below, we will use both means and medians, each to their own purposes.

To keep things clear, we remind the reader (and ourselves) once more that the mean or median Weedmaps price of an eighth of flower or a gram of oil doesn't include the extra state and local cannabis taxes and other sales taxes imposed at the cash register. That means the actual prices paid by consumers are higher than the prices we report, and in some places much higher.

Different States, Different Prices

So legal American weed often costs in the neighborhood of $40 as an eighth of flower or a gram of oil, plus tax. But this price is hardly constant across the United States. Like weed laws, legal weed prices vary a lot by state. In this section, we show you some inter-state price differences from our data.

We do not report any price statistics from states with only a few retailers because we have no way to know if the samples of prices in those states reasonably represent the state as a whole. But even after we narrow the field to the states with the most data, there are 19 states we can look at in different ways.

We mentioned that ⅛ ounce of flower and 1 gram of oil are comparable amounts of weed as measured by THC potency. In Table 4 and Figure 17, we take advantage of this similarity to look at the differences between prices for ⅛ ounce of flower and for 1 gram of oil in 12 different states for which we have both Weedmaps retail price data and Cannabis Benchmarks wholesale farm price data.

Table 4 shows mean farm prices, mean retail prices, and retail-to-farm price ratios (mean retail price divided by wholesale farm price) for ⅛ ounce of flower and 1 gram of oil. By *farm price*, we mean the price paid to the cultivator (grower), typically by a distributor, for bulk flower transfers. The 12 states are sorted from lowest to highest by mean wholesale farm price.

On the question posed by Table 4—Where's the cheapest legal weed at the farm?—Colorado wins, edging out Washington and Oregon. But other patterns in Table 4 also jump off the page.

First, there is a wide range of farm prices: from less than $9 in Colorado to more than $32 in Illinois for the same (mostly) raw

TABLE 4. Where's the cheapest legal weed at the farm?

Farm and retail prices for ⅛ ounce of flower and 1 gram of oil in 12 U.S. states, October 2021.
Ordered from cheapest to most expensive mean farm price.

State		Region	Recreational sales began	Mean farm price[a] ⅛ oz flower	Mean retail price ⅛ oz flower	1 g oil	Retail-to-farm price ratio[b] ⅛ oz flower	1 g oil
CO	Colorado	West	Jan 2014	$8.88	$30.13	$43.90	3.4	4.9
WA	Washington	West	Jul 2014	$9.03	$37.23	$39.81	4.1	4.4
OR	Oregon	West	Oct 2015	$9.12	$32.67	$32.51	3.6	3.6
CA	California	West	Jan 2018	$9.34	$43.99	$48.93	4.7	5.2
OK	Oklahoma	West	Not yet	$13.56	$30.48	$30.61	2.2	2.3
AZ	Arizona	West	Feb 2021	$14.40	$43.54	$62.69	3.0	4.4
NV	Nevada	West	Jul 2017	$15.76	$48.32	$58.50	3.1	3.7
MI	Michigan	East	Dec 2019	$18.41	$45.28	$41.40	2.5	2.2
ME	Maine	East	Oct 2020	$20.61	$34.61	$41.16	1.7	2.0
AK	Alaska	West	Nov 2016	$24.94	$47.72	$82.49	1.9	3.3
MA	Massachusetts	East	Nov 2018	$28.22	$51.36	$95.01	1.8	3.4
IL	Illinois	East	Jan 2020	$32.27	$59.73	$101.45	1.9	3.1

Sources: Cannabis Benchmarks (October 2021 wholesale data); Weedmaps (October 2021 retail data).

[a] Price paid to cultivators for bulk flower transfers. Multiply by 128 to get price per pound.
[b] Mean retail price divided by mean farm price.

material. Compared with the bulk farm prices of other agricultural commodities, these are very big differences between states—a reflection of the fact that legal weed can't be freely traded (or "arbitraged") across state lines without breaking state and federal law and risking arrest. (Quick caveat: farm price is highly correlated with potency, and it may be that farm weed in Colorado has lower average THC than farm weed in Massachusetts and Illinois, whose weed is more likely to be grown indoors.)

Second, there is also wide variation between states in how much legal weed prices get multiplied along the supply chain between grower and consumer, through the steps of distribution, testing, packaging, labeling, and retailing. The second and third columns of numbers in Table 4 show retail prices. Now Oklahoma leapfrogs the other western states and has the cheapest retail oil and almost the cheapest retail flower.

The rightmost two columns of Table 4 show retail-to-farm price ratios for flower and oil in all 12 states in this sample. (Note that the two are not directly comparable to each other, since there are additional processing steps involved in distilling flower into oil, manufacturing cartridges, etc.) We also note that weed oil is also processed from leaves that are "trimmed" from around the flowers during the process of preparing flowers for the retail market. These leaves have lower THC per gram but are dense enough to be marketed for production of oil, if not for smoking directly.

For flower, retail-to-farm price ratios range from a low of 1.7 in Maine (so the retail flower price is 70 percent above farm price) to a high of 4.7 in California (where the retail flower price is 370 percent above farm price). Maine also has the lowest retail-to-farm price ratio for oil (2.0), and California has the highest (5.2). Maine has relatively high farm prices but just middle-of-the-road retail prices. So Maine's retail markup ratio is the lowest of all states we looked at. California, on the other hand, has relatively low farm prices but high retail prices. The high California markup reflects, at least partly, the high cost of doing distribution and retail in California—not just weed distribution and retail, but any kind of distribution and retail.

The third thing to notice in Table 4 is the association between the date when legal recreational sales began and the mean farm price. Each state in our sample is on its own time frame, and some have been wrestling with legal weed for a lot longer than others. In general, farm and retail prices are lowest in the states that legalized earliest. Colorado, Washington, and Oregon were the first three states in America to open legal recreational weed stores, and they have the three lowest farm prices in America. This pattern could be related to the fact that the growers that have been legal for the longest have had the most opportunity to adjust to the constraints of the new legal market, optimize their businesses, and build economies of scale over time. It may also be that these are states, along with California, that have significant outdoor weed production, and outdoor weed tends to be cheaper.

Table 4 also shows an apparent association between farm price and region. The seven states with the cheapest farm prices in the contiguous U.S. are all west of the east edge of Texas. The four states with the most expensive farm prices in the contiguous U.S. are all east of that line. In all, the average farm price of flower in the eight western states is $13.13 per eighth, or $1,680 per pound. The average in the four eastern states is just under twice as much: $24.88 per eighth, or $3,185 per pound.

Why such a difference? Well, for starters, outdoor weed is the cheapest weed, and Illinois, Massachusetts, Michigan, and Maine are not hospitable climates for outdoor weed. (Same deal for Alaska, which is outside the contiguous U.S. but also has expensive prices.) On the other hand, in most states, greenhouse and indoor weed, combined, make up considerably more of the market than outdoor weed, so climate effects can't explain this whole difference. Regulations and bureaucratic barriers to entry also likely play a role, but we have not yet studied carefully the data comparing the costs or effects of regulations in East Coast states versus West

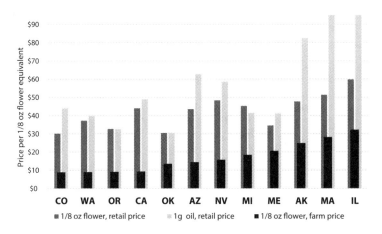

FIGURE 17. Mean prices in 12 U.S. states for retail cannabis flower, retail cannabis oil, and flower at the farm. States are listed in order from lowest to highest farm price (in US$); ⅛ ounce of flower and 1 gram of oil are each equivalent to about 0.7 grams of pure THC. Sources: Cannabis Benchmarks (July 2021 wholesale data); Weedmaps (July 2021 retail data).

Coast states. Later in this chapter, however, we do explore this issue a bit more through the lens of Oklahoma.

In Figure 17, which illustrates the data in Table 4, we look at the differences between retail prices for ⅛ ounce of flower, retail prices for 1 gram of oil, and farm prices for ⅛ ounce of flower, which are all prices for roughly the same amount of pure-THC-equivalent weed. Plotting farm and retail prices on the same set of axes helps illustrate the farm-to-retail price ratio and how it varies between states.

The Highs and the Lows

For each of the thousands of retailers listing prices in our data set, we also looked at the lowest price on the menu and the highest

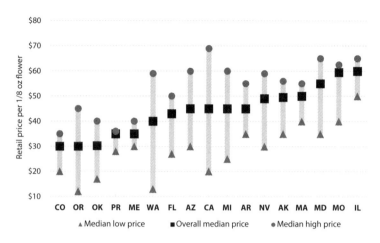

FIGURE 18. Median low price, overall median price, and median high price at retailers for ⅛ ounce of cannabis flower in 17 U.S. states (including Puerto Rico). States are listed in order from lowest to highest overall median price (in US$); ⅛ ounce of flower is equivalent to about 0.7 grams of pure THC. Source: Weedmaps (July 2021 retail data).

price on the menu for each package quantity and product: for example, an eighth of flower or an ounce of oil. Then we calculated the median lowest price and median highest across all sellers in each state. This gave us a window into what consumers pay for low-end, bottom-shelf weed and high-end, top-shelf weed in each state.

Figure 18 provides a visual representation of the highs and lows: the median high price, median low price, and overall median price of ⅛ ounce of flower in 17 states with at least 1,000 price listings from at least 20 retailers for this product type on Weedmaps.

What we notice in Figure 18 is the wide variation in the ranges between median low and median high prices. Some states, such as

Colorado, Maine, Massachusetts, and Illinois (and Puerto Rico), have relatively small ranges, meaning that the median low price is not much lower than the overall median price and the median high is not much higher than the overall median price.

Some other states, such as Oregon, Washington, California, and Michigan, tend to have bigger ranges of low to high, with lower lows and higher highs. These states with big spreads are scattered along the range of overall median prices. We do not yet have enough evidence to make claims about the causes of these effects.

Where's the Cheapest Legal Weed?

Next, we ask: Where's the cheapest retail legal weed in America?

The cheapest way to buy weed at a legal retail store is to buy it by the ounce of flower, and to buy the cheapest ounce of flower at the store. Table 5 rank-orders states by their median prices for the cheapest 1-ounce flower packages listed at each retailer. Prices for low-end ounces of retail flower vary between states even more than prices for median eighths of retail flower.

In Table 5, we show median low prices for two package sizes of weed: 1 ounce, the cheapest flower package on a per-gram basis; and ⅛ ounce, the most common flower package. We show prices in each of the 19 U.S. states (including the territory of Puerto Rico) where our data set had at least 50 prices from at least 10 unique retailers for both of these package types. Of these 19 states, 12 (shaded in gray) are recreational and 7 are medical-only. In Table 5 we also convert these low-end prices to grams so you can directly compare the price per gram of 1-ounce and ⅛-ounce packages. The list is ordered by cheapest to most expensive for 1 ounce of flower.

TABLE 5. Where's the cheapest legal weed at retail?

Median retail prices for 1 ounce and ⅛ ounce of flower in 19 U.S. states and territories with at least 50 1-ounce price listings, 50 ⅛-ounce price listings, and 10 merchants. Sorted in order of median low price for 1 ounce of flower, low to high.

State		1 oz of flower		⅛ oz of flower	
		Median low price	Per gram	Median low price	Per gram
WA	Washington	$60.00	$2.14	$13.00	$3.71
OR	Oregon	$64.10	$2.29	$12.00	$3.43
OK	Oklahoma	$90.00	$3.21	$17.00	$4.86
CO	Colorado	$100.00	$3.57	$20.00	$5.71
CA	California	$139.00	$4.96	$20.00	$5.71
MI	Michigan	$150.00	$5.36	$25.00	$7.14
ME	Maine	$180.00	$6.43	$30.00	$8.57
AZ	Arizona	$185.00	$6.61	$30.00	$8.57
NV	Nevada	$185.00	$6.61	$30.00	$8.57
PR	Puerto Rico	$199.50	$7.13	$28.00	$8.00
MT	Montana	$200.00	$7.14	$30.00	$8.57
MD	Maryland	$220.00	$7.86	$35.00	$10.00
AR	Arkansas	$252.00	$9.00	$35.00	$10.00
NM	New Mexico	$255.78	$9.14	$35.00	$10.00
IL	Illinois	$271.64	$9.70	$50.00	$14.29
AK	Alaska	$280.00	$10.00	$35.00	$10.00
MO	Missouri	$295.15	$10.54	$40.00	$11.43
MA	Massachusetts	$300.00	$10.71	$40.00	$11.43
HI	Hawaii	$330.00	$11.79	$45.00	$12.86

Source: Weedmaps (October 2021 retail data).
Shaded states = Legal recreational sales.

One basic result in Table 5 jumps off the page: Washington and Oregon are the cheapest states in America to buy cheap weed, by a fair margin. Washington's median low retail price of $60 per ounce of flower—equivalent to $2.14 per gram, or $960 per pound—is well below the mean *farm price* of flower in most U.S. states. Oregon has both the cheapest median retail eighths of flower ($12 per eighth, or $3.43 per gram) and the second-cheapest low-end ounces of flower ($64.10 per ounce, or $2.29 per gram) in America. For both 1-ounce and ⅛-ounce packages, Washington and Oregon low-end prices are considerably lower than the prices for any other state.

Oklahoma is the other headline story here, standing out from the rest of the medical-only states with some of the cheapest weed prices in the country. Oklahoma's median low price for a full ounce is the third-lowest in the country and less than half the median low price in any other medical state.

What is striking, especially in comparison to other agricultural product markets, is the difference between the top and bottom. Massachusetts and Hawaii have median low prices for 1 ounce of flower that are $300 and $330 per ounce ($10.71 and $11.79 per gram), respectively—five times Washington and Oregon's median lows of $60 and $64.10 per ounce.

You'd have a hard time finding another legal agricultural market in North America where low-end prices in one state are five times lower than low-end prices in another state. Even for perishable, delicate products that don't ship well, like eggs, the cheapest products in the cheapest states aren't five times cheaper than the cheapest products in the most expensive states. The biggest spreads between states that you see in other agricultural markets are for products where special standards (e.g., environmental or animal-welfare rules, like mandatory cage-free eggs) are imposed in one state and not another. But even when California imposes a cage-free egg standard, California can still import cage-free eggs from Iowa if it's cheaper to produce cage-free eggs in Iowa, and an arbitrage opportunity arises. Interstate commerce limits interstate price differences. Weed can't be legally transferred between states, so the lack of legal arbitrage may be the single biggest reason there's such a big spread between states in the price of the cheapest weed.

Where is the cheapest low-end oil?

We don't include this in our numerical tables, but we'll answer the question. The cheapest packaged retail price per gram of oil (not including bulk oil) is typically found in a 1-gram cartridge. The lowest prices are in Oklahoma, where the median low price for a 1-gram cartridge, which, recall, is roughly equivalent in THC to ⅛ ounce of flower, is just $21.18. This works out to $2,711 per pound of flower—significantly more (unsurprisingly, given the added processing costs) than Oklahoma's farm price of $1,735-per-pound legal flower.

Oregon comes in second with the median low-end 1-gram oil cartridge costing $24. Washington is a close third with the median low-end 1-gram oil cartridge costing $25.

Where's the Most Expensive Weed?

We next turn to the most expensive. We won't tire out your eyes with more tables, but we'll give you the headlines.

The most expensive package of flower, per gram of flower, is the smallest widely available package: one gram of flower. (We're not counting prerolls, nor do they figure into our retail flower price estimates in this chapter, since they are technically manufactured products in their own category.)

The most expensive high-end flower in America is found in California, and it costs two dimes: $20 for a gram. That's about $70 per eighth, $560 per ounce, or $8,960 per pound—almost five times the price of a low-end gram of flower in Oregon ($4.20). Illinois (also with a median of $20 per gram, but with a mean of $26 compared to California's mean of about $29) comes in second for most expensive high-end flower.

But the most expensive weed of all isn't flower. A small (half-gram) package of high-end oil is most expensive in Missouri, at $80 per 0.5 grams. This works out to $160 per ⅛ ounce flower equivalent (about 0.7 grams of pure THC), $1,280 per ounce, or $20,840 per pound. In second and third places for most expensive high-end oil are New York and Pennsylvania ($75 per half gram of oil).

General Patterns and Anomalies in U.S. State Differences

One general pattern that emerges from Tables 3 through 5, and Figures 17 and 18, is that the trio of states that first established legal recreational sales (Colorado, Washington, and Oregon) are all states with cheap legal weed. In these states, legal retailers are able to give illegal retailers the most spirited competition.

On the other end of the spectrum, the heroic median prices for the cheapest possible eighth from a seller in Hawaii ($45) and Illinois ($50), about four times what low-end eighths cost in Oregon ($12), suggest that the many consumers on tight budgets in Boston or Chicago are probably looking outside the legal markets for their weed.

Toward the bottom of the list in low-end price is California, the world's biggest legal weed market, where the lowest price for an eighth is above only three other states (Oklahoma, Washington, and Oregon). One might expect the enormous amount of competition, innovation, and talent in the state to be driving low-end prices down even further, but the cheapest weed currently costs about 70 percent more in California than it does just over its northern border in Oregon ($20 versus $12). California has high prices for many low-end goods, and weed is no exception.

Partly as a result of these not-that-cheap low-end prices, California's legal weed market is relatively small. We estimate that less than 30 percent of the weed that is bought by consumers within the state, by weight, is legal, and more than 70 percent is illegal. It's pretty safe to say that this is not what the California voters had in mind when they voted for Prop 64, or what the state government had in mind when it implemented Prop 64. There are lots of reasons for high legal prices and low legal share of sales in California, and a few of them show up as examples in later chapters.

Oh My, Oklahoma!

On the flip side, there is Oklahoma, a medical-only state with four million residents whose legal medical weed industry did not launch until October 2018. As of October 2021, three years later, Oklahoma had one retailer listing on Weedmaps per 3,060 people in the state—easily the most retailer listings per capita of any state in our data set.

What has made Oklahoma so successful at keeping legal weed prices low and availability high? Many possible factors may contribute to a vigorous legal weed industry. In addition to a notable per capita density of retailers in Oklahoma, the state has the lowest farm price and lowest median retail price of any medical-only state in America—and some of the lowest prices of any state, recreational or medical. The median Oklahoma price for low-end weed by the ounce is just $90, or $1,440 per pound. Only Oregon ($64.10) and Washington ($60) are cheaper.

The combination of high per capita retailer density, lots of product variety per retailer, and low retail prices makes logical sense: a more competitive market means lower prices that are closer to marginal costs. However, it's also important to keep in mind that Oklahoma's consumer prices are generally low compared to other states. The state has relatively low land, labor, and other resource costs, and businesses face less extensive regulations than they do in many other places in the United States. So it is relatively cheap to run any kind of business in Oklahoma, and a typical box of pasta at a supermarket in Oklahoma is priced lower than its counterpart in California or Massachusetts. Still, the differences are bigger in weed.

Oklahoma, land of sooners and cowboys, may not be perfect weed-growing land, but it's definitely farmland. Politicians and regulators may be farmers or other business people themselves and tend to make regulations easy to follow for other farmers and business people. In this regard, Oklahoma may be an outlier in the U.S. legal weed landscape. A variety of licensing and testing requirements are in place, but they were determined and written in a way that makes compliance highly feasible. Perhaps most importantly, the licensing authorities in Oklahoma are known for being fast-moving and responsive, granting licenses within days.

It is hard to overstate how Oklahoma legal weed has flourished. Oklahomans voted to legalize medical weed on June 26, 2018, passing a ballot question called SQ 788 by a 57 to 43 percent vote. The first legal medical dispensary in Oklahoma, the Tulsa Higher Care Clinic, opened the morning of June 27, the next day, about 12 hours after polls closed. This world record for shortest time between voting to legalize weed and first legal weed sales in the state may stand forever.

In the weeks and months that followed, the Oklahoma legislature decided not to schedule a special session to set up detailed regulations. Instead, a looser system was put in place that simply adhered to the requirements of SQ 788. No limits were placed on the number or location of weed businesses. No local approval was needed. Applying for a weed license wasn't so different from applying for a hunting or fishing license.

By December 24, 2018, six months after the Oklahoma ballot question passed, more than 2,000 business licenses had been granted to 799 dispensaries, 1,284 growers, and 336 processors, and the state had already collected $8 million in license fee revenue. In its first full year of regulated operation, 2019, Oklahoma retail weed sales were about $350 million, about $89 per state resident. In year two, Oklahoma more than doubled its first-year retail sales, to $830 million.

Vermont, by contrast, legalized recreational weed on January 22, 2018, five months before Oklahoma voted for its medical-only legalization. As of mid-2021, three and a half years later, the Vermont state government still hadn't collected a dollar on recreational weed or allowed a single recreational retail store to open. Vermonters may end up taking four years to do what Oklahomans did in half a day.

It's also worth mentioning that Oklahoma's demand is not limited to Oklahomans. Texas, which doesn't even have a medical weed program to speak of, has a long border with Oklahoma, and a lot of retail weed sold in Oklahoma ends up in Texas. Although Colorado is more convenient to Texans in that it has recreational weed and doesn't require a state medical recommendation,

Dan's First Foray into Weed Economics

By Dan

When I was a kid, a rite of passage for young empirical economists was to practice using statistical methods to estimate "parameters" and test hypotheses. It was like a finger exercise to learn technique before actually making the beautiful music of real research.

Step one is gathering some data. My classmate and buddy Joe suggested that rather than examine dry bean supply in Michigan or something equally mind-numbing, we should gather data on the big farm commodity that no one had yet studied.

This was the early 1970s, and no one had done serious statistical economics on weed. As we learned, the U.S. Department of Agriculture had (and still has) no data on weed production. Since no other typical sources had anything either, we decided to conduct a survey of weed farms to gather information on acreage, inputs, and weed output to allow us to study the production relationships.

Joe is from Georgia and I am from California—our research was bicoastal. We had siblings still on the family farm. We knew growers and guys who knew growers.

We carefully prepared a set of questions and the cover letter on official university letterhead. As with all such surveys, even those about dry beans in Michigan, we promised confidentiality of the data and no attribution to any specific farm. We mailed out dozens of surveys, each with a stamped return envelope enclosed (it was the 1970s).

We got zip, nada, nothing. Not even Joe's brother would respond. Our eventual research paper was about economic theory and econometric methods, and that was the end of my weed research for about four decades.

When the California weed regulators asked me and Robin to study economics of weed regulations, I recalled my first foray, and my immediate response was "No, sorry, I just don't do drugs anymore."

there are plenty of Oklahomans with friends in Texas and even some who make a living hauling goods to friends south of the border.

The first medical weed dispensary you hit in Oklahoma driving up I-45 from Texas is called Border Buds, in Thackerville. It's located 2,500 feet from Texas, 1,500 feet from the Oklahoma State Line Monument, and an hour and a half from Dallas. Border Buds gets 4.7 stars on Google, and charges about $20 for an eighth of flower. It's a bright peppermint green modular home with the word "dispensary" painted across its side in the biggest letters you've ever seen on a shack. It's open 24/7, and you can't miss it from the Interstate, even if you try.

Which States Have Made the Most on Weed?

In the last part of our data discussion in Chapter 4, we turn to overall sales by state. We gathered tax revenue data from five western U.S. states that are comparable in many ways: Colorado, Washington, Oregon, Nevada, and California.

In Figure 19, we compare side by side their economic fates by showing aggregate legal weed retail sales (total number of dollars spent by consumers) by quarter in each of these five western states since recreational legalization began. We have not yet undertaken a more detailed analysis of the different outcomes in these five western states, but we can observe some broad trends in their overall retail revenue.

The five states have much in common, including recreational legalization, previously existing medical weed industries, a history of exporting weed, and favorable outdoor growing conditions (Nevada is the exception to the last three rules).

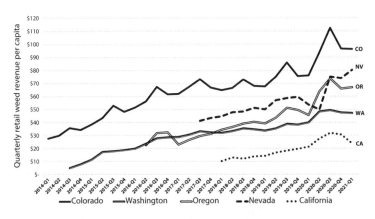

FIGURE 19. Total legal weed retail sales in five western U.S. states since recreational legalization.

Given these similarities, the size of the differences between states in legal weed revenue per capita surprised us. California is known in popular mythology as queen of weed, producing and consuming prolific amounts of it in-state and exporting more than half of America's illegal supply for decades. Yet California, among its cohort of legal-weed neighbors, has been far behind its neighboring states in total revenue per capita from legal weed for the full three years since regulated weed launched in 2018.

The numbers plotted in Figure 19 are quarterly. States (especially Colorado and Washington) typically show bumps in the third quarter of each year (back-to-school weed?), so the curves are not so smooth. Overall, Colorado ($96 per quarter per state resident) and Nevada ($80 per quarter) top the Q1 2021 charts, with Oregon in third place at $67 per quarter, Washington in fourth at $47 per quarter, and California bringing up the rear at $24 per quarter.

The spirited performance of Colorado and Nevada in Figure 19 might have something to do with their big tourist industries. The

FIGURE 20. MedMen ad on a Las Vegas taxi. Credit: Robin Goldstein.

denominator in the fraction that determines per capita sales is the number of state residents, not the number of people in the state at any given time. It's well known that people from all over the world go to Colorado to snowboard and to Vegas to sin (Figure 20). Weed often accompanies both of these activities, and in some states with recreational legalization, as in Amsterdam for generations, weed itself may be turning into a tourist attraction.

Did COVID-19 Lockdowns Affect Weed?

From spring 2020 through spring 2021, COVID-19-related lockdowns across North America affected the weed industry, as they affected many other industries. Weed retailers (like off-premise alcohol retailers) fared relatively well throughout the pandemic.

Some people reported seeing an uptick in weed sales during the pandemic, when everyone's sitting around at home all day with nowhere to go. Do the data support this? We took a look.

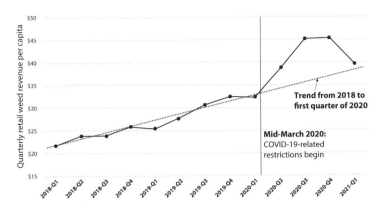

FIGURE 21. Aggregate legal weed retail sales in five western U.S. states (CO, WA, OR, NV, and CA) during COVID-19-related restrictions.

First, this COVID-19 bump shows strongly in Figure 19 above, which displays a third-quarter (Q3) 2020 jump in all of the five western states. The patterns are mixed otherwise, so we next consider the aggregate of the states.

Figure 21 shows weed sales between the first quarter of 2018 to the first quarter of 2021, in the combination of all five western states with recreational legalization that are separated out in Figure 19 above. Again the states are Colorado, Washington, Oregon, California, and Nevada. The dots in Figure 21 above represent *aggregate* quarterly sales (all five states put together). The sudden bump you see in the 2020 lockdown-affected time periods of Q2 through Q4 (April through December) is consistent with an impact of lockdowns on sales.

There is much more to do to test the COVID-bump hypothesis in a statistically rigorous way, but we also note that when you trace a trend line (using a linear regression) from Q1 2018 to Q1 2020, before the pandemic hit, the line traces to a point that's right around Q1 2021, suggesting that the COVID-19 bump might have come back down to earth by spring 2021.

In the next chapter, we'll give you a break from the data, numbers, and charts, we'll turn to stories from our home state, and we'll take you on California's long, strange trip through legalization.

5   *California Dreamin'*

In 1996, California became the first state in America to legalize weed for people with medical permissions. This chapter tells the strange but true story of our own state's gory encounter with economic reality as we finally lurched into recreational legalization 22 years later. Other states that are earlier along the legalization process now have the luxury of looking back and learning from many things California learned the hard way.

California's first set of rules for medical weed, established under Prop 215 of 1996, didn't say much. They didn't explicitly legalize the sale or distribution of weed. They simply made it legal for patients and designated "primary caregivers" to possess and cultivate marijuana for personal medical use given a doctor's recommendation. Primary caregivers were defined as people responsible for the housing, health, or safety of patients. In the early days, many growers mistakenly assumed that they could qualify as caregivers simply by providing medicine to patients, even in a so-called buyers' club that sold weed to thousands of members.

Police, sheriffs, and DAs strongly disagreed and busted many growers and clubs. Courts sided with law enforcement, ruling that primary caregivers had to assume a personal, consistent responsibility for patients' welfare. While patients could legally share and grow weed for themselves, they couldn't buy or obtain it from clubs or stores.

The 420 Era Begins

The general confusion over Prop 215, and the generally tight restrictions on how to obtain legal weed, were not addressed at all by lawmakers until 2003, a full seven years after Prop 215, when an act of the California State Legislature called SB 420 (wink wink) set some more, and more tolerant, rules for the oversight of legal medical weed.

Some readers may not know that the number 420 is a slang reference to weed. Hence April 20 is a big weed holiday in some places. The term 420 was originally invented by a group of students at San Rafael High School (just north of San Francisco) known as the Waldos, who used to meet at 4:20 p.m. to smoke weed.

In a crucial but vague provision, SB 420 authorized patients to organize "collective" or "cooperative" cultivation projects on a nonprofit basis. A host of "patient collectives" promptly sprouted up around the state selling weed to patients on a walk-in membership basis. In theory, collectives could charge for the cost of their labor and supplies but not rake in a profit.

SB 420 was kind of a compromise bill that gave some framework for what the state would and wouldn't prosecute in terms of commercial marijuana cultivation and retail operations, and what it meant for these dispensaries to start opening. But the most important thing to know about SB 420 is what it didn't do: regulate or authorize commercial sales. The state chose not to set up a system of licensing, taxation, and regulation for Prop 215 collectives.

Neither Prop 215 nor SB 420 ever established any system of state licensing, taxation, or other active state regulation of Prop 215 collectives, other than to say that the weed activities described would not be prosecuted as crimes by state law enforcement. California's weed market existed in a legal purgatory, in the space between the cracks in all of the regulatory systems that exist for almost every other kind of product. People in the California industry often refer to the years following 2003 as the "420 era."

At the very beginning of the 420 era, it was largely medical patients who were buying and selling weed under these laws. But after a few years, the medical weed system started to expand well beyond the initial medical patients. Starting in the late 1990s, a small number of patients, and a growing number every year since then, had started getting doctors' recommendations and going to retailers where they could buy weed in a commercial environment. Many weed consumers showed a preference for going to retail stores that felt similar to conventional retail stores.

In spite of the growing medical system, most people in California, before and after 420, probably kept buying weed as they always had, from their local dealer. In California as everywhere else, the illegal weed market was thriving in the early 2000s, bolstered by an increase in fashionable use by students and young professionals. At the same time, legal medical dispensaries that looked a lot like retail wine stores started popping up in more places and serving a wider audience. People started smoking weed in mass-market Judd Apatow movies, network TV series, and almost every single hip-hop video recorded from 2001 onward.

Alongside the growth in illegal and legal medical retailers was a growth in "weed docs," who started opening offices and offering Web services everywhere in the state. These medical doctors specialized in writing recommendations for medical weed patients. Getting a recommendation got a lot easier as walk-in clinics proliferated and competed on price, speed, and willingness to recommend weed for almost any claimed ailment. The clinics had names like "420 Docs," staffed by a combination of retired hippie doctors and marginal or disgraced doctors.

Under the rules, doctors' letters did not recommend specific products or dosages and therefore authorized patients to buy anything in a legal medical weed store. Given the flexibility of doctors and the breadth of conditions that doctors felt weed could treat, the state had no power to stop the medical market from becoming a de facto recreational market.

Even as legal weed became easy to access for California buyers, it never got easy for out-of-staters to buy legal weed. Virtually all storefront retailers in California implemented tight controls on doctors' permission letters, including checks on the date of the recommendation letter (which had to be updated annually) and the credentials of the doctor signing the letter. The prohibition against sales to out-of-state residents was observed religiously, whether for fear of enforcement or by convention.

The Brown Doctrine Is Established

In 2006, a few years after SB 420, the California weed industry was reshaped, gently, by the attorney general ("A.G.")'s guidelines, also informally referred to by some as the "Brown Doctrine" after then-attorney general Jerry Brown, who signed the document. To some extent the A.G.'s guidelines specified what medical weed dispensaries could and couldn't do and what corporate forms dispensaries could take (collectives or cooperatives).

But the A.G.'s guidelines, like their predecessors in California weed law, were vague, and they carried much less force than an act of the state legislature. Legally, the guidelines were little more than a memo with some nonbinding suggestions. A dispensary had to verify the California ID, verify the medical permission, and not violate local zoning and business laws. But it was never clear what the specifics of the rules for weed businesses really were, because there were no statewide regulations governing weed during that long period in California. This lack of guidance was especially pronounced for the many independent growers who supplied the retailers with their weed.

At this point in weed history, businesses at every level, but especially growers, were still constantly fearing federal raids. In the eyes of federal law, running a dispensary with dozens of pounds of weed on hand is still the official equivalent of being a drug kingpin like Pablo Escobar. As of the mid-2000s, the federal government was still actively raiding weed businesses and hauling their owners, operators, and even janitors into federal prison.

With the federal "Cole Memo" in 2008, another nonbinding document, the U.S. Department of Justice at the end of the Bush administration indicated that their federal agents were going to take a step back from these raids, without expressly taking away their right to conduct them. If you were a cannabis business following state and local laws and not doing anything else wrong, the Feds said they were not going to spend money on prosecuting you just for your state-compliant marijuana activities.

Under the California A.G.'s guidelines, medical collectives and cooperatives were to be organized as nonprofits. However, nonprofit is a corporate form that doesn't prevent you from making operating profits: nonprofits can have big operating profits and then basically pay out those profits to their employees in the form of large salaries, or in many cases divert the profits into holding companies or auxiliary businesses that are owned by the same companies, and so forth. There are many ways to get money out of a nonprofit into the hands of an executive, operator, or owner of a for-profit holding company.

The medical marijuana industry really started picking up steam in California in 2004 and 2005, and practically speaking, it busted open the ever-fuzzier medical/recreational distinction, which became little more than a rule that limited sales to state residents. Your friends didn't care whether you used weed medically or recreationally. Your real doctor didn't care. Your weed doctor, of course, made a good living with very little effort, because anyone who wanted to consume legal weed with the state needed a written permission.

Socially, in the early 2000s, the taboo about weed fell away in California sooner than it did anywhere else. Vapes and spliffs replaced or enhanced Chardonnay at bachelorette parties and after-work happy hours. People in California started talking about weed more comfortably around their parents and their kids. Students and professors were smoking weed together in the middle of creative writing seminars at UC Santa Cruz. (We can't substantiate this claim, but if you ever visit the UC Santa Cruz campus or talk to a former student from 1970 to 2020, you will likely agree that it probably happened at some point.)

To some extent there was a parallel in Washington and Oregon. The whole U.S. West Coast was ahead of the rest of the country. In terms of density and popular acceptance of weed retail stores, most of the U.S. East Coast in 2020 has progressed to where California probably was in about 2005.

Proposition 19: Still Too Soon?

Fourteen years after medical legalization, in 2010, California made its first major effort to legalize adult-use cannabis. The campaign was led by Richard Lee and Dale Sky Jones, the founding members of the legendary Oaksterdam, a center of cannabis industry, culture, and education in the heart of Oakland that was modeled after the coffeeshop culture of Amsterdam. Working with a team of local advocates, Jones and Lee spearheaded and led funding for a recreational legalization measure known as Proposition 19 (the Regulate, Control and Tax Cannabis Act of 2010), which qualified for the California ballot. The proposition and its proponents, probably wisely, used the term *adult-use* for what we usually refer to as recreational, and *cannabis* for what we call weed.

Although some people from NORML—including its California director, Dale Gieringer—had reservations about Prop 19, NORML supported the measure. NORML was especially sensitive to the devastation of communities that criminalization of weed and other drugs had contributed to.

Prop 19 would have made California the first state in America to legalize recreational weed, which many expected, given the state's history of being first to legalize medical weed. But on November 2, 2010, Prop 19 failed by a vote of 54 to 46 percent.

We do not even pretend to know how to predict politics or read elections, but it is important (and fun) to lay out the process of legalization that continues to expand, and some of that is fascinatingly inseparable from politics, especially in California. Some inside accounts give a flavor of the varied views of some of the pro-weed lobbyists in California over the course of two legalization ballot initiatives: the unsuccessful one in 2010 and a successful one, Proposition 64 (the Adult Use of Marijuana Act), in 2016.

Because of the failure of Prop 19, it was not California but Colorado and Washington, in 2012, that became America's first states to vote for the legalization, taxation, and regulation of recreational weed.

The Hippies Regroup

There was plenty of blame to go around among those who had supported Prop 19. Some media pointed to a coordinated last-minute effort by evangelical churches, especially in Orange County and rural areas. But Dale Gieringer of NORML, whom we introduced earlier, thinks a bigger problem was that the pro–Prop 19 effort was premature, running in an off-year election when left-wing turnout is normally low. Gieringer also thinks the provisions of Prop 19 were ill designed to attract moderate voters with little interest in the topic.

The evangelical church community was only one of several forces working against Prop 19. An even more powerful one was law enforcement. Local police forces across California were getting contingent funding where they were paid extra—directly compensated by state and federal funds—on the basis of their numbers of drug arrests and convictions. There were strong individual and collective financial incentives to arrest small-time weed criminals for possession or small-time sales. A secondary but also important factor was that weed possession laws gave law enforcement a pretext for arresting people whom they suspected of other crimes, or whom they didn't like hanging around on the streets. (When recreational legalization and licensing eventually arrived, this problem never quite went away, as there are still plenty of unlicensed sellers around for police to arrest if they want to.)

Making the 2010 election harder was the recognition that there were about 10 million citizens in California of the sort who reliably vote and who had for 30 years supported a broadly conservative agenda of Republican governors from Reagan forward. Demographics and politics have changed enough in California to make 2010 seem like a long time ago. In 2010, many of the pro-weed activists and supporters had the precise profile of people who do not actually show up on election day. One may not need conspiracies about police funding or powerful churches to explain a simple overreach by activists who were out of touch with and still could not read the voting public.

Dale Gieringer, at first glance, looks like your typical Oakland bohemian in his 70s, with a trimmed gray beard and a mischievous smile. He claims that he is not an ex-hippie, although we have not verified this fact independently. Beneath the unassuming surface is one of the world's wise men of weed. His book *Marijuana Medical Handbook: Practical Guide to Therapeutic Uses of Marijuana* is a bookshelf mainstay of just about every medical weed practitioner in California. After meeting Gieringer, you immediately intuit that he has not been bought. He tells stories from the heart. You would never know that he is a Harvard graduate.

Gieringer admits to being more of a policy wonk than a fundraiser. Although fundraising was never his job, he is critical of today's wealthy cannabis investors for failing to help out in the earlier efforts or the 2010 campaign to make cannabis legal.

There is a misperception that weed activists want legalization so that they can buy weed more easily. Trust us: weed activists already have access to all the great, cheap weed they could possibly want. Nor are they heavily invested in the weed industry financially, nor could most of them afford to be even if they wanted to.

For the most part, the activists have been advocating not on their own behalf, but on behalf of prisoners. Activists believe deeply that weirdly stringent antiweed laws and discrimination in enforcement created generations of nonviolent prisoners and generations of poor or marginalized children, many of them minorities, who grew up with imprisoned or unemployed parents. The result was uncountable damage to communities. This rationale for legalization may not have quite the political sway over Californians that Gieringer and his colleagues wish it did, but it is powerful nonetheless.

A New Coalition Arises, Then Fragments

After the 2010 loss, the pro–Prop 19 coalition re-formed and expanded to plan for a 2016 initiative. Leaders of California's pro-legalization groups met on a regular basis to discuss and work out the details of a new ballot initiative and campaign strategy. Dubbed the "Coalition for Cannabis Policy Reform" (CCPR), the new group was led by Prop 19 campaign director Dale Sky Jones, Cal NORML director Gieringer, and some attorneys, consultants, and representatives of California's legal medical weed industry, including Steve DeAngelo, founder of Oakland's famous Harborside dispensary. For the sake of branding and brevity, CCPR dubbed their initiative campaign "ReformCA." There were a lot of weed-savvy people in the group, a lot of big egos at the table, and a lot of different ideas.

A common understanding developed within the group that 2016 would be the year for the next initiative. But that was about the only thing the growing group of weed luminaries could agree on. By mid-2015, things had started getting weird, and the prospect of getting the necessary signatures still seemed distant. A rival group, led by Lynne Lyman of the Drug Policy Alliance (DPA) and Graham Boyd of the New Approach political action committee, broke away from the ReformCA coalition and began working on an initiative of their own. On almost every major aspect of the statutory material being drafted, DPA disagreed with the ReformCA approach.

DPA was a national organization that had supported ballot measures in other states, and they came in with significant money. Gieringer says that the DPA approach was to try to put a weaker legalization initiative on the California ballot—"weak" meaning conservative, restrictive, and making concessions to whatever groups were necessary to achieve success (even if the laws resulted in excessive obstacles for businesses to enter the legal recreational market). DPA and like-minded allies wanted to assure the largest possible electoral margin for recreational legalization—regardless of the downstream consequences.

After the defection of DPA, a major rift developed in the whole community of cannabis activists in California who wanted an initiative on the 2016 ballot. Some people switched sides. Close friends were competing to raise money from the same sources for different organizations with the same stated purpose. At one point it looked like there might actually be two rival legalization initiatives on the ballot, as sometimes occurs in California. That would have meant befuddled voters, chaos in the media, and the likely failure of both initiatives.

Getting a proposition on the California ballot is typically just a matter of hiring a huge army of young people to stand around shopping malls and street corners and go door to door to get citizens to sign a nice-sounding petition about which they generally have no clue. But it takes millions of dollars to do that. As 2016 approached, with support split, neither ReformCA nor the DPA group was raising enough money to get the needed signatures.

To get on the 2016 ballot, either of the pro-weed interest groups would have needed orders of magnitude more money, fast, to hire armies of people to canvass streets all over California—not to mention the TV ads to defeat the evangelicals, law enforcement groups, and other antiweed interest groups that had helped bring down the 2010 bill.

In Comes the Savior from Big Tech

In swooped an unlikely figure: Sean Parker (Figure 22), founder of Napster (the file-sharing service that started the peer-to-peer revolution in violation of intellectual property law and managed to stick around for years before getting shut down) and the first president of Facebook. Parker had something that nobody in either rival pro-weed coalition did: he was really rich and knew other really rich people.

Parker didn't quite come out of nowhere. He had previously dabbled in the Prop 19 effort and had been lurking in the background of the legalization effort for a while. He declined to meet with Dale Sky Jones and ReformCA but had begun behind-the-scenes discussions with DPA. One big reason DPA and Graham Boyd separated from CCPR was that they realized Parker had the money to get the job done—and the contacts too: California governor-to-be Gavin Newsom was aware of Parker's efforts, and Parker was a major contributor to Newsom's campaign.

FIGURE 22. Sean Parker. Credit: Kathy Hutchins / Shutterstock.com.

For the 2016 election, Parker was committed to designing a new initiative himself and funding the whole thing if necessary. And so Proposition 64, the Adult Use of Marijuana Act (AUMA), was born.

Parker's ideas were a lot more similar to DPA's initiative than ReformCA's initiative. By election day, Parker had brought a lot of influential people to his side and put in far more money than anyone else. According to *Forbes*, Parker donated $8.9 million to the three main groups funding the ballot initiative. Other billionaire donors included Hyatt heir Nicholas Pritzker II (of Tao Capital Partners and cannabis software company MJ Freeway) and PayPal cofounder (and well-known conservative libertarian) Peter Thiel. This was not the ReformCA crowd. The libertarian-leaning billionaires also seemed like an odd bunch to support the high taxes and elaborate industry regulations that were at the core of Prop 64.

Even haters admit that, from the start, Parker's intentions appeared to be noncommercial. Parker was a weed smoker who believed prohibition to be unjust, and he did not seem to have financial interests in any weed companies. Far from being corrupt, Parker seems to have had the opposite problem: almost everyone who told the story of Prop 64 complained that Parker had almost no contact with members of the $2-billion-per-year legal (medical) weed industry in California. It is unclear whether Sean Parker had ever grown weed, but it is clear that nobody, or almost nobody, in the leadership of his organization knew much about how the weed industry operated in California.

Members of the ReformCA group, on the other hand, had deep experience in the existing medical cannabis industry in California. ReformCA was working with NORML, which had fought their legal struggles for decades, and trade groups to which farmers, distributors, and retailers belonged. There were plenty of people in ReformCA who knew how to grow weed and how the medical marijuana supply chain worked. But nobody on any side seemed versed on how commercial farming and the supply chain worked for other farm commodities.

This was a 2016 California weed industry that was, by some measures, thriving. There were more than 3,000 weed retailers across the state, including thousands of delivery services for customers who did not want to go to the store in person. It took 10 minutes on a website to get a doctor's permission and five minutes on another website to schedule your delivery. The legal market was large and growing. (Of course, the illegal weed market was even larger and also growing.)

People were coming from all over the country to hang out with their friends in California and try the fabled California weed. Everyone knew someone with a medical card, so if their consumption was not quite legal, at least the weed came from a legal joint. College and high school students had no problem getting it (just like beer).

California's medical weed industry was vibrant in other ways too. New products like gummies, tinctures, vape pens, and dab rigs were aimed at an expanding and increasingly segmented market. Successful industry participants reported that their margins were high and demand was healthy. For farms, processors, retailers, and many consumers, the need for "legalization" was not related to the industry's performance.

In the 2016 California market, as in today's market, a very large segment of total weed production and consumption was sourced from suppliers who made no pretense of complying with medical retail rules and whatever farm and supply chain rules there were, if any. And a big chunk of California farm production, then as now, was shipped as illegal weed to out-of-state buyers.

Illegal retailers in California were also doing well. Illegal sales to California customers were a big share of the local market. Lots of farm producers supplied both weed sold at legal dispensaries and weed sold by "independent" merchants who did not bother checking for medical cards or other identification or complying with local rules if there were any. The illegal retailers also skipped paying sales taxes and other trappings of standard legal businesses. Many people in the broad weed industry did not want *any* change in the way things worked, and many insiders, especially those in the illegal industry, opposed Parker's efforts.

Of course, that was one of the selling points of Prop 64. It was not really pro-weed, it was pro–legal weed. Supporters claimed it was designed to make business *harder* for the illegal weed industry. When the illegal industry complained, that was a sign that the ballot measure might actually accomplish one of its goals. Politically, Prop 64 was sold as positive for law enforcement and for getting rid of bad guys.

Compromises Are Made

One of the guiding principles of ReformCA had been that any proposition should benefit, not harm, the preexisting legal medical weed industry. On the other hand, Parker's approach seemed to ignore rather than support the preexisting industry, legal or illegal. Nothing in the text of Prop 64, from production to distribution to retail sale, seemed to be informed by how the legal weed businesses in California actually did business. Instead, Parker's text created new ways of doing weed business at every level of the supply chain. With its regulatory complexity, Prop 64 made all preexisting weed businesses in California illegal on day one and offered them the opportunity to enter a new, very different, highly regulated industry. As a consolation, preexisting weed businesses got priority processing of their license applications, if they were actually able to qualify and submit an application.

It was probably a poorly informed fantasy to think that existing businesses could just continue as before, or make minor adjustments to comply with the new rules. The medical weed industry had no statewide regulations and a light touch on monitoring even the informal rules. The industry was simply far out of the mainstream of California business regulations. After two decades of almost no statewide rules for legal medical weed, in late 2015, when recreational legalization appeared to be on the horizon, the California legislature approved a package of bills known as the Medical Marijuana Regulation and Safety Act (MMRSA) to comprehensively regulate the existing medical weed industry. MMRSA was then adopted as a model for the regulatory provisions in Prop 64.

Besides elaborate regulations, Prop 64 added taxes aimed at raising $1 billion in revenues. Under Proposition 64, the whole supply chain was to be taxed and regulated much more extensively than any other farm-based businesses, even wine. Most in the California weed business understood this, which is why, when faced with reality, they preferred to stay illegal and off the grid.

Parker did not seek the support of ReformCA people. He only communicated with them at the last minute, while seeking to head off the nightmare of two competing petition campaigns. At any rate, ReformCA didn't have the funding to proceed. Many of the orphans of ReformCA and allied groups eventually agreed to back

Parker. In the first two weeks of December 2015, according to *MJBizDaily*, at least seven board members defected from ReformCA to Parker's coalition. Steve DeAngelo also jumped on board with Parker.

Gieringer stayed fast with CCPR, although he ultimately endorsed Prop 64 on account of its provisions decriminalizing weed offenses. During the entire process, Parker never granted CCPR a single in-person meeting. Word on the street was that you had to contribute a lot of money to the cause if you wanted to get a seat at the Prop 64 table.

In retrospect, one can see why the CCPR crowd was not of much use to Parker. A relatively unfunded group of known weed advocates had little leverage to sway mainstream voters. The people and organizations who could afford this buy-in were mostly special interest groups outside the weed world, and they were politically useful. Legal handouts written into Prop 64 went to public health organizations, treatment programs, youth education programs, water drainage and other environmental groups, antipesticide lobbyists, the NAACP, the California Narcotic Officers' Association, and, in a massive way, the Teamsters Union. A central feature of Proposition 64 (and another vestige of the 2015 MMRSA law that the California State Legislature had passed to regulate medical weed) was a complex and cumbersome three-tier system modeled after the unique, and uniquely inefficient, U.S. alcohol regulation system that was first put in place after the repeal of alcohol prohibition in 1933.

The end result of all the input was a long and complicated proposition that hardly a single voter would have read or could have understood. ReformCA's proposed statutory language was 26 pages long; Prop 64's was 62 pages long. Particularly unsupported and undiscussed within the industry, by several accounts, was the tax structure set up in Prop 64, which imposed taxes at two different stages: an initial cultivation tax of about $148 per pound and an excise tax initially set at 15 percent of a theoretical but unmeasured "retail price," which worked out, initially, to 24 percent of wholesale price.

Under Prop 64, local jurisdictions were also guaranteed the freedom to impose unlimited local taxes, at all stages of the supply chain, on top of the state cultivation and excise taxes. In this respect California was different from Massachusetts, for instance, which passed a ballot measure in the same year that capped local weed tax at 3 percent of retail revenue.

Some of Prop 64's most important features related to regional diversity and law enforcement. The key "local control" or "local option" provisions of Prop 64 provide that any city or county in California has the right to ban weed businesses from its jurisdiction. Local control was a key feature of MMRSA. Prop 64 adapted MMRSA's local-control model to recreational regulation.

Under Prop 64's local-control provisions, permission from local officials was made a prerequisite for any business to receive a state cannabis license, but local officials were not required to issue such permissions to weed businesses, even in jurisdictions that had not banned them. This enabled local sheriffs and police to maintain de facto prohibitions on local weed businesses and continue to arrest people for involvement in commercial weed activities in their jurisdictions.

The major, and bitterly controversial, exception was that people in jurisdictions that banned legal weed businesses could still order legal weed from delivery services in nearby cities or counties that hadn't banned legal weed—albeit with longer delivery lags, and with availability limited to the delivery services that were willing to travel longer distances.

On November 8, 2016, Proposition 64, the Adult Use of Marijuana Act, passed by a vote of 57 to 43 percent, with many features that the old marijuana activists hated.

Say what you will about Sean Parker: he got it done. Maybe a ballot proposition like ReformCA's would also have passed that year, but we will never know. Parker did it quickly, expensively, and with a package supported by many disparate groups with little agreement about much else. In the process, he brought on board environmental lobbyists, labor groups, the health care industry, and other parties whose demands he and his partners did not fully understand. He made compromises with law enforcement that some activists thought were unacceptable.

The mission of many activists was to spend as much as it took, and do whatever it took, immediately, to stop imprisoning people for weed. Many in America have spent nights crying over someone who was taken away from the people they loved, over weed. In the 20 states that have yet to act, no policy is more central to the disproportionate imprisonment of otherwise innocent people for nonviolent offenses that the majority of the American population don't consider to be offenses at all.

The mission of Sean Parker and the rest was not only to liberate these "offenders" and bring them home to their grieving families, but also to restore their rights, expunge their convictions, and qualify them for jobs where they could support their families and live normal lives. These were the priorities. The details were sidelined. The people who did it must be applauded And here we are.

Self-Fulfilling Paranoia

Almost every regular weed consumer, at some point in his or her life, reports having had a paranoid feeling induced by weed. On the first night when Robin knew he had finally felt the effects of weed, he stared at himself in the mirror for more than an hour in an attempt to convince himself, unsuccessfully, that its effects were ever going to end.

What exactly is paranoia, and what does it mean to say that it is induced by the drug?

Paranoia is an ungrounded feeling that something bad will happen, or that people are out to get you. When you are paranoid, you are locked in a grip of fear that does not respond to reason. This happens. Most people have experienced paranoia at least a few times, with or without drugs.

Yet it can also be reason, an overabundance of reason maybe, that first generates the fear and thus paranoia that can come with drug use. How do you know whether the paranoia comes from the drug, or from drug education, or from the prospect that the policeman you're passing on the sidewalk could potentially arrest you for drugs?

Wherever drugs are prohibited, once you're doing or possessing drugs, it immediately becomes *true* that they're out to get you. It's no longer a paranoid thought. It's just the reality. Your paranoia has actualized.

Even as weed is legalized—much faster than many people thought likely—it still might take generations to separate the consumer experience of weed, and the associated paranoia, from our lifetime experience of weed's illegality.

6   Sabrina's Story

Around 2009, Robin signed up for the newsletter of an organization called the National Organization for the Reform of Marijuana
Laws (NORML). He started getting regular email missives from
someone named "Sabrina at NORML," which he would eagerly
devour when they arrived. The newsletter would inform Robin of
the progress of various ballot initiatives or legislative acts to legalize medical or recreational weed around the country.

From the start Robin was deeply sympathetic. Of all the coun-
terproductive U.S. government policies in his lifetime, Richard
Nixon's 50-year-old War on Drugs and its angry uncle, mass imprisonment, had always seemed like the most vicious. Weed, the light-
est of the major narcotics in terms of effects and punishments,
ended up becoming the workhorse pawn of the War on Drugs.
Weed's smallball game has been responsible for more arrests,
especially of young people of color, than all the other illegal drugs
put together.

By 2008, someone was being arrested for a weed offense every
37 seconds in the United States, and the U.S. reached a new mile-
stone in the War on Drugs: our 20 millionth weed arrest. Although
an increasing number of states had voted for and implemented

legal systems for the production, sale, and use of medical weed, even the most compliant businesses were in constant danger. Federal agents were routinely seizing the homes and freezing the life savings of medical weed business owners even if they were compliant with state law.

For almost all of Robin's adolescence and most of his adulthood, NORML has been opening the public's mind by stating simple facts like these. People at NORML speak and act from the heart, and that has always been a fundraising obstacle and probably a limit on mainstream media appeal.

As a then-recent graduate of one of the most left-wing law schools in the country, Robin at the time supported every one of these efforts. Not that he actually did anything else about it, other than forwarding the messages from Sabrina at NORML to his schoolmates. Robin and most of his schoolmates and friends were naive and distracted followers, not activists. But almost all of them, pot smokers and squares alike, supported with all of their hearts, from the comfort of armchairs, the vague idea of freeing nonviolent drug criminals from jails and prisons across the United States— people who are disproportionately poor, disadvantaged, and minorities. They would support *any* initiative and *any* legislative act that would help liberate prisoners for nonviolent weed crimes.

There are more living Americans who have tried weed than have not. How could something most of us have done be not just a crime but an imprisonable crime? Is there anything else that most Americans have done that is imprisonable, in some places and some cases, for life?

For activists and their followers, including Robin, activism around legalization has always been most about bringing home the two or three or generations of people unjustly imprisoned in the

War on Drugs. But for the grace of God and the stolen gift of privilege, many more of us would have lost our freedoms. The idea behind the activism of the early 2000s, real and armchair, was to make compromises and just get legalization done in a way that would liberate the prisons. That was objective number one, everything else was a distant second. It was the right thing to do.

But for many, now is the time to worry about the secondary consequences of the way things were done.

It turns out that unlike Alexa from Amazon or Siri from Apple, Sabrina from NORML is a real person who is really named Sabrina: Sabrina Fendrick (Figure 23). The daughter of two US diplomats, Sabrina grew up all over the world and finished high school in Arlington, Virginia, just outside D.C., the center of the U.S. lobbying universe. She stayed in the area during her time at NORML's D.C. headquarters when she was Robin's email correspondent.

Sabrina has been working since January 2015 in California as an executive with Berkeley Patients' Group (BPG), the nation's oldest, continuously operating (now recreational) dispensary. Immediately after starting at BPG, she was thrown into the legislative process in 2015 working on the initial Medical Marijuana Regulation and Safety Act (MMRSA), which became the foundation for the 2016 ballot measure legalizing adult use. In 2020, Robin tracked her down and asked her how she felt about Prop 64, two years after implementation.

"The best thing to come out of Prop 64," Sabrina said, "was the mechanism and the mandate to clear records and the drop of arrest rates. But I don't know anybody that's making a profit in the cannabis industry. Some people are breaking even. Nobody's making a profit." Before Prop 64 was implemented in 2018, Sabrina said, "the legal industry in California was doing pretty well. It was really

FIGURE 23. Sabrina Fendrick. Credit: Jennifer Skog / MJ Lifestyle Magazine.

coming up. There was wide participation. . . . Now it's basically just in a constant state of survival. I know plenty of people who regret going into the legal market."

Why has the legal industry set up under Prop 64 been so unappealing for the businesses with which Sabrina is familiar and sympathetic?

"The biggest thing," says Sabrina, "is the price point. It's become so clear to me that there are two means of availability for consumers in California. One, the illegal market, is a lot cheaper and a lot more accessible than the other, the legal market. Prop 64 intended to get rid of the illegal market. But the authors of Prop 64 failed to consider these market forces. They made the taxes and licensing barriers too high. . . . Where there are legal channels available, the cost of a cannabis license, rent, taxes, compliance expenses, all of it adds up and it is too expensive. So that also makes the prices of the products higher. The bottom line is that illegal weed is still cheaper and more accessible in a majority of places than the legal weed."

In particular, the local control option—the option to prohibit the production and sale of local weed (see Chapter 5)—turned out to be a beast. Local control was initially viewed by many as a minor concession that would be exercised only by local jurisdictions in very conservative areas. Instead, local control was exercised widely and had a powerful effect.

Many of the people who voted in favor of Prop 64 on the state ballot took a more conservative approach when it came to their own cities or neighborhoods and supported various forms of local control. The activists like to call these types of voters "NIMBYs": Not In My Backyard, a term often applied to those who contest locations of businesses with negative local impacts, such as farms or shopping. To keep out activities that may negatively affect local amenities, many people justify local zoning ordinances that are broadly popular in California, especially on the privileged left. The collective results stunned many: under local control, three-quarters of California's land area implemented total prohibitions on weed businesses.

Before Prop 64, medical weed businesses had not required state licenses, only local licenses, if that. Assuming that the businesses observed state laws about medical recommendations and so on, they were de facto legal (on a state level). Some jurisdictions had no medical weed retailers, but before the approach of Prop 64, relatively few had passed blanket bans on them. On a local level, medical weed businesses that observed other zoning laws and didn't unduly disturb neighbors had been tolerated by most local officials.

But when Prop 64 came along, and with it the prospect of recreational legalization and even weed tourism, many city officials or county boards of supervisors passed total prohibitions. Many areas that had previously had legal retailers—such as Marin County, a small, wealthy left-wing enclave just north of San Francisco— became legal weed deserts (except for delivery operations willing to deliver from a different county), leaving the territory more available for the illegal market. As with alcohol prohibitions, local control became the illegal market's best friend.

Local prohibition of production and sale, says Sabrina, "creates a vacuum that's filled by something because there's a demand. The supply is still moving through, just not through legal channels. The secondary [illegal] track has thrived. You have such a wide spectrum of the illicit market. It's not just Mexican gangs or illegal dealers; it's also former people that ran collectives, medical practitioners. The illicit market is made up of a diverse range of sellers."

In a market sense, what Sabrina calls the "secondary track" was always primary, and "legalization" did not change that. Two years after legalization, of more than 10,000 weed growers that were thought to exist in Humboldt County, only a few hundred had applied for licenses from the California Department of Food and Agriculture. It is not clear how many of those 10,000 were ever "legal" under previous laws, regulations, and taxes that have covered farms and other businesses for decades. The markets and business relationships before November 2016 remain murky. What is very clear is that Proposition 64 did little to shift much weed from illegal to legal. In many specific cases it did the opposite.

Recall that in California and other places with legal weed, consumers break no law by buying and using weed from an illegal seller. That is, when we say "illegal weed," it is the supplier, not the product supplied, that is illegal. Many consumers do not know or care whether their weed supplier is licensed or unlicensed (no testing, taxes, or government quality control). So, says Sabrina, even in places where there are plenty of legal weed retailers the illegal market is still a powerful force: "Anyone can find off-market or legacy weed. Because it's cheaper and networks are well established. Legal cannabis is not really affordable for a large percentage of California. Consumers can buy their $200 ounce before tax from the licensed market, or $100 per ounce from the unlicensed market. What do you think they're going to do?"

The old-line activists were concerned but had not predicted the extreme and disproportionate impact of local control or understood the way complications for legacy weed suppliers were written into almost every paragraph of Prop 64. They had not predicted that becoming legal would be insurmountable for so many previously existing businesses.

"I was used to looking at language about criminal justice, parental rights," said Sabrina, referring to her time at NORML. "I didn't know then how to read language for operational impact as well as I do now. Later I realized how little I knew as an activist about how hard it is to operate a cannabis business. I wish I had been more critical and engaged in the drafting process." But Sabrina, in spite of the role she had played earlier in the process, was not even in the room during the drafting of Proposition 64— and she wasn't part of Parker's inner circle—so it is not clear where her input would have been welcomed.

In 2021, more than three years after Prop 64 regulations were implemented, California had less than one-third the number of weed retailers listed on Weedmaps than it did in 2017, before Prop 64 regulations took effect. But that statistic understates the actual business attrition, because the new total includes many newly opened businesses. By our calculations, fewer than one in 10 California medical cannabis retailers that had been listed on Weedmaps in 2016 were still on the site in 2018.

Figure 24 shows attrition of retailers from Weedmaps in seven California counties (Butte, Fresno, Kern, Los Angeles, Sacramento, San Diego, Santa Clara) between September 2016 and August 2018, based on data we collected over that 21-month time period. You can see the drastic decrease in retailers around January 2018, when enforcement of the new Prop 64 regulations began.

For many activists, one of the most heartbreaking provisions in Prop 64, which had been a major priority of ReformCA, NORML, and others in the traditional weed community, was the lost right to smoke weed in public. Prop 64 banned weed

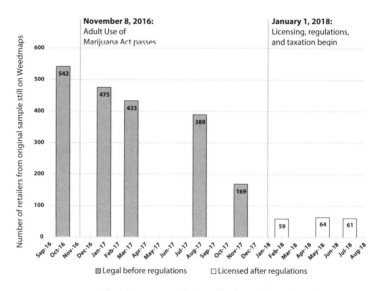

FIGURE 24. Attrition from a panel of medical weed retailers after recreational legalization: number of cannabis retailers still listed on Weedmaps out of an original sample of 542 retailers in seven California counties that were listed in September 2016.

smoking—and, even more surprisingly, vaping—in public places across the state, even areas where tobacco smoking is allowed. Although there is little evidence that this rule is being enforced, in principle consumers are permitted to consume weed only in private homes or at state-licensed weed events, which are rare. So under Prop 64, neither a homeless person nor a hotel guest can legally consume weed anywhere—so much for weed tourism. A soldier who lives on a military base, which is federal property, also has no place to smoke weed. Before Prop 64, there was no statewide ban on the public consumption of weed, and (in the absence of a specific local ordinance) medical patients could legally smoke weed anywhere they could smoke tobacco.

At midnight on January 1, 2018, the night that Prop 64 regulations went into effect, NORML's Dale Gieringer says: "We celebrated. It was like celebrating on the *Titanic*. A group of us went out at midnight to protest. For 22 years, it had been legal for us to smoke on the sidewalk. Until midnight that night. We went out to smoke a protest joint. It was civil disobedience."

For the many unexpected effects of Prop 64, Sabrina puts some of the blame on herself and her fellow activists. She believed deeply in the cause, and she was great at her job of lobbying lawmakers, but she says, "I realized how little I actually knew about inner workings of a cannabis business. How expensive it was, the cash situation. I hadn't actually realized how language can completely change how a business operates. Sometimes for good, sometimes for bad."

"I was bright-eyed and bushy-tailed," says Sabrina. "Coming from NORML, it was very humbling for me to see how much I didn't know about the supply chain. Being a consumer advocate, I had been focused on arrests and criminal implications. NORML dealt a lot with operators that got raided out in California and in other states. I could see how the activists like me didn't understand business implications. The movement was started by activists and grew out of that spirit. Now I realize there were so many things we weren't considering, especially how interconnected consumer advocacy and an accessible, quality-controlled supply chain really are. The illegal operators need an incentive and mechanism to come over. Otherwise why would they? Why would they stop meeting that demand? I'm not an economist—it's just human nature. How do you want to encourage behavior? You need to create an environment that is welcoming and empowering."

These days Sabrina has become a leading expert in commercial cannabis and taxation policy. She continues trying to learn from other parts of the country about how weed could be regulated more effectively. Ex-activists are wondering whether Oklahoma, which has a medical-only system with comparatively restrained regulations—simple license applications and fast processing of applications—has hit on the right formula for legal weed, or for legal anything. When the bluest of blue-state liberal activists are looking to red states for guidance on regulatory policy, you know something's gone haywire.

But weed economics are hard for almost anyone to figure out. When you try to legalize weed and accidentally end up illegalizing it instead, it's important to have a very open mind about what to do next.

How Do We Fix It?

And so we come to the heart of the discussion about the larger effects of the high costs and prices of legal weed. If having a big illegal weed market and a small legal weed market in a state after recreational legalization is a problem, then what, if anything, can be done to fix it?

One solution is to ramp up raids on illegal operations and try to eradicate them by stricter law enforcement. But this is often described as a game of "whack-a-mole." Every time one illegal operation gets shut down, two more open.

It also seems pretty clear that in most of the country, people have no more stomach for the mass imprisonment of people growing and selling weed that is legal to buy. Law enforcement raids of illegal weed cultivators and sellers, like the one shown in Figure 25, tend to

FIGURE 25. A bad day for a cannabis cultivator.

work against central goals of many of the people who voted for legalization and the activists who fought for it, like freeing nonviolent poor people from prisons and reuniting them with their families.

Imprisoning tens of thousands of people in America, mostly poor, mostly minorities, and giving criminal records to hundreds of thousands, created negative ripple effects across the country for nearly a century after cannabis prohibition began in the 1930s. The larger economic and noneconomic effects of imprisonment are powerful and hard to quantify—like the psychological effect on children who grew up without a mother or father because of the laws that criminalized weed possession and made small-scale sale a major crime punishable by many years in prison. So it's easy to see why so many activists were so eager to pass recreational legalization by any means necessary.

But some activists thought they could have the best of all worlds: regulate legal weed so thoroughly that you make it perfectly safe, bring in lots of tax dollars to the state, make entrepreneurs rich, eliminate the illegal weed market, and make the new system inclusive of the formerly illegal operators who suffered under criminal laws that are viewed by today's lawmakers and citizens as unjustly harsh.

Recreational legalization has brought none of the above, anywhere in North America.

The Private Equity Hustlers Lose Too

Ultimately the joke was also on the suits, the Harvard University and Yale Law School graduates running well-capitalized funds, because almost none of them have made money in legal weed either. There just haven't been enough consumers willing to pay enough for legal weed to cover the suits' capital costs, their lawyers, and their consultants.

Tens of thousands of growers, most of them consultant-less, continue operating in the shadows (literally, because of their need to shield their weed canopy from surveillance), sustaining a North American illegal weed market that may be as healthy as ever.

What the activists and the "ganjapreneurs" both had a hard time foreseeing was that beyond a certain point, regulating legal weed more strictly, and making costs and prices even higher, might be worse, not better—for the legal weed market and for the community as a whole, for the rich and for the poor.

Aspirational Laws

Apart from economic outcomes, some social theorists believe that it's generally bad for a supposedly civil society to be full of people

FIGURE 26. The aspirational speed limit.

who are constantly breaking laws. For instance, one argument against having a 55-mile-per-hour speed limit (Figure 26) that isn't really enforced, such that almost everybody goes 70 or 75, is that it breeds disrespect for laws and rules in general. The idea here is that observance of the laws by citizens is a "public good" that yields hard-to-quantify benefits to society in the safety, harmony, and long-term sustainability of a community. So it might be optimal to raise the speed limit to a level that people are actually likely to obey, and enforce it consistently.

You can call rules that nobody follows "aspirational" rules. We like to believe that they are being followed, but they aren't. Just because you post a "Speed Limit 55" sign, and somebody in the government aspires to the ideal that nobody drives over 55, doesn't mean it actually happens on the highways.

Similarly, just because you make and tightly enforce rules for legal weed to follow, and somebody in the government aspires to the ideal of all weed becoming legal, doesn't mean that legal weed actually defeats illegal weed in the marketplace.

We want you to come away from this chapter, and this book, with the recognition that economic incentives of buyers and sellers mean that legal weed and illegal weed must compete with each other. Things that make it harder and more costly for legal sellers (and buyers) help the illegal industry. Sabrina understands this lesson and its implications clearly.

A buyer's choice between legal weed and illegal weed responds to the *relative prices* of the two goods. If you create a new safety regulation or a higher tax that makes legal weed even more expensive, for example raising the price from $45 to $50, and illegal weed meanwhile keeps its price (almost) unchanged, some consumers will predictably respond by substituting: replacing some of their legal weed with illegal weed. This will make the legal weed market quantity smaller and the illegal weed market quantity bigger.

So a clear takeaway from this chapter is that an attempt to make legal weed safer and more closely regulated can actually shrink the legal market and grow the illegal market through the high costs of legality and the barriers to legal market entry. This effect, in turn, may result in other side effects that many people view as negative, like more criminal activity in general and less observance of the law by the citizens.

The Good News

What would help make legal weed cheaper to produce, lower retail prices to a level closer to illegal weed, and enable legal weed to become competitive in price in the long run? Time, for one thing. Recent evidence of legal weed costing $75 per ounce for retail buyers in Washington and Oregon is good evidence that the wisdom (and trial and error) of the years can eventually bring competitive prices.

Regulatory changes can also bring change sooner. Policy makers can relax access restrictions, extend legal hours of operation, relax certain security regulations, lower tax rates or licensing fees, or remove the power of local authorities to prohibit or limit the number of weed businesses within their jurisdictions. Simplifying the licensing process could make legal weed cheaper in many places and allow a fuller range of small businesses to enter.

Of course, it's a lot easier to write the ballot question or the legislation right the first time around than to change rules once they're made. So there may be a reason to think Tennessee, Kentucky, and the other states that are moving at their own much slower pace may learn something from the trial-and-error process in California and elsewhere. They have had opportunities to study the foibles of other states, like the stories we tell in this book, as they work through their early drafts. The best such discussions among policy makers, we like to imagine, would center less on what it is prudent to license, regulate, monitor, and tax than on what it is prudent *not* to license, regulate, monitor, and tax.

Legalization or Illegalization?

We have covered a lot of the economic effects of recreational weed legalization, but another big effect has been the sudden and rapid increase in the number of weed-related crimes being committed in recreational legalization states in the wake of the sudden increase in the number of weed-related laws in those states. Ironically, U.S. states with recreational legalization may have more criminal weed operations running, and more criminally punishable weed activity occurring, in terms of violating state law (e.g., operating without a license), than they did in the early 2000s, when medical weed was in its infancy, or even before that, when all weed was illegal.

And this is why some people say—and we consider it plausible—that the so-called "legalization" of weed in some North American markets has illegalized more weed than it has legalized.

7 *Legal Weed in 2050*

We now turn to the legal weed market 30 years in the future, around 2050. By then, we expect that there will be a mature, vigorous market where weed is legalized and regulated nationally in the United States, traded between U.S. states, and probably traded among the U.S., Canada, and Mexico.

A central question we consider in this chapter is: Are typical prognosticators right about the long-term future market for legal weed, or are they high?

Most observers agree with the basics of the long-term expectations we just listed, including national legalization and probably international trade. With that starting outline, lots of industry representatives, analysts, forecasters, and media observers promise the moon. They see a rapidly expanding pie and a huge amount of money that will be shared by all sorts of legal weed businesses in the future (Figure 27).

Typical analysts simply project, on the basis of early percentage growth rates and a few assumptions, that the revenue generated in the U.S. (and international) legal retail weed market will become vastly larger decade by decade. And many project that national

FIGURE 27. A next-gen weed label printer printing thousand-dollar bills. Credit: Robin Goldstein.

legalization will help almost all legal weed businesses by allowing better access to capital and a much bigger market.

In 2018, the San Francisco market research firm Grand View Research projected a $146 billion global cannabis retail market by the end of 2025. In 2020, Cowen & Co., another major player in the space, projected an $85 billion retail market by 2030 in the United States alone.

Using the economic principles and background data developed in previous chapters, we now take our own turn looking into the future. We look at the cannabis industry in 2050, further out than most analysts. As you will see, we differ from them in other important ways, and we end up with dramatically different conclusions.

Some prognosticators come up with dramatically different conclusions than their own past selves: as of 2021, the same Grand View Research folks who in 2018 had projected a $146 billion market in 2025 are now projecting a $91.5 billion market in 2028. We say: good for them, better late than never, and 2025 is uncomfortably close.

Before laying out our assessment about future prospects, we want to make an admission that you seldom find among forecasters. We are probably wrong. There are lots of ways our projections may go astray, and at least one of them is likely to occur. But bear with us. Whether we turn out to be right or wrong, we hope you will appreciate our approach and gather facts and notions that are useful to any effort to think through the future of legal weed.

We start by stating and exploring four expectations about big changes we see ahead for the cannabis industry. The first two changes relate to laws and regulations, and the third and fourth changes relate to technology and business developments. All four expected changes might (on the surface) sound positive for the industry, and they tend to be given a positive spin in the media.

We find all four changes to be quite plausible and even highly likely. After these four changes are incorporated into the market, we expect that weed will eventually develop into a normal mainstream industry. We find their consequences interesting, and probably uncomfortable for many current weed businesses. The four big changes are:

1. U.S. national legalization and regulation of weed
2. Legal interstate and international weed trade
3. More efficient weed farm production and processing technology and practices
4. Real agribusiness: scale, specialization, financing, and management improvements

We'll now look at each of these four expected changes in the context of what we have already discussed in previous chapters about weed regulation, taxation, farming, technology, and business management. We'll uncover how the four expected changes affect the likely path of revenue of legal cannabis business.

Expected Long-Run Change #1: U.S. National Legalization and Regulation of Weed

As of 2021, under U.S. federal (national) law, weed is a Schedule I illegal narcotic—a designation reserved for substances with "no currently accepted medical use and a high potential for abuse" under the Controlled Substances Act of 1970—bringing the laws in all 30 to 40 legal-weed or decriminalized-weed states into conflict with federal law.

The federal legalization of weed is a major change that seems like a matter of time, and the time is almost at hand. Here we use the term *federal legalization* the way that some others use *federal decriminalization* or *descheduling*, meaning the removal of weed from the U.S. Drug Enforcement Administration (DEA)'s list of Schedule I illegal narcotics. Along with this federal change, weed legalization is likely to continue to spread in all (or effectively all) states and local jurisdictions.

Much uncertainty and political complexity surrounds the timeline for federal legalization. The process could take anywhere from one to five or even fifteen years. But we predict that full federal weed legalization, and probably regulation and taxation, will happen well before 2050. Recent momentum suggests a faster timetable. Some think the schedule for federal legalization should be considered in months, not decades.

An additional step beyond this, which could not occur sooner than legalization but could occur way after legalization, is what we call "federal regulation": the introduction of a federal system of licensing, taxes, and standards. Such a system could look similar to or different from the one we have for alcohol.

Mere federal legalization, without federal regulation, would make life easier for the legal weed industry in some ways. The federal prohibition on weed currently creates a variety of problems for weed businesses that are operating legally under state laws. These problems include weird income tax rules and highly restricted access to the banking system. The IRS, under its infamous Section 280E, prohibits weed buyers or sellers from deducting most business expenses, resulting in huge tax liabilities. And banks with protection from the FDIC (Federal Deposit Insurance Corporation) are prohibited from lending to businesses engaged in federally illegal activities, including weed. Some of this is what prompted the *Standing Akimbo* legal case from Colorado that Justice Thomas wanted the U.S. Supreme Court to review (see "Weed Supreme" later in this chapter).

But federal legalization would surely not help everyone in the industry. First, it would probably imply interstate commerce (expected long-run change #2), which means the same type of interstate market that is guaranteed by the Commerce Clause of the U.S. Constitution for legal products. Trade economists know that not everyone wins from free trade. As we discussed above, the basics tell us that producers and suppliers in high-priced places may sell less or even go out of business when markets are opened. Also, states with especially costly regulations would find competitive pressure to relax some regulations to help local businesses compete with out-of-state sellers.

We think federal decriminalization or legalization could lower weed pretax wholesale prices and retail markups to such an extent that the total value of legal weed markets could decrease substantially even if the quantity of legal weed produced rises a lot. How could that happen?

A big unknown here is whether, and how, the federal government chooses to regulate the weed industry. If an additional layer of federal regulations and taxation is imposed on top of state taxes (as is currently done for alcohol), or if federal barriers to licensing are high, then an unknown number of additional costs could be added, further jeopardizing the legal market's chances for success. In that case, legal weed quantities would likely fall, driven by rising after-tax costs at retail.

Consider the example of federal taxes on booze. U.S. taxes on alcoholic beverages are fixed per unit of alcohol. They are not set as a percentage of price. That means alcohol taxes are a big deal for cheap booze but have little effect on fancy wine or on alcohol bought in bars and restaurants, where the retail markup is high. A similar approach to weed would have important implications everywhere. Depending on the level of federal taxes and whether they were laid on top of state and local taxes, the implication could be to make cheap legal weed relatively more expensive, to the benefit of cheap illegal weed.

Expected Long-Run Change #2: Legal Interstate and International Weed Trade

One part of federal legalization would almost surely be interstate competition in weed. This is so important and so misunderstood that we want to highlight it separately.

As of mid-2021, 18 U.S. states (plus the District of Columbia) had passed legislation or voter ballot initiatives to legalize recreational weed; 12 of these had set up legal frameworks to regulate the recreational industry; and 36 states had passed legislation or voter ballot initiatives to legalize medical weed. These numbers are changing quickly. In the medical-only states, a wide range of standards govern the circumstances under which patients may legally be permitted to use weed.

The Commerce Clause of the U.S. Constitution (Article I, Section 8) prohibits states from using laws that impede the free exchange of goods between states unless states have a compelling public interest in impeding such free exchange. However, the Commerce Clause does not protect the interstate trade of federally

Weed Supreme

Which U.S. Supreme Court justice has been most supportive of legal weed over the past two decades?

The answer—or ours, anyway—might surprise you.

In the U.S. Supreme Court's famous 2005 decision in the case *Gonzales v. Raich,* the Court allowed the U.S. federal government to prosecute two California women for growing and using medical cannabis in accordance with California law. The Court held that the women's growing weed at home and consuming it as tea to mitigate cancer symptoms was tantamount to interstate commerce, so the Feds had the right to bust into their homes and dump out their tea.

The majority decision was supported by both right- and left-wing justices, including Antonin Scalia and Ruth Bader Ginsburg. Against the majority and in defense of legal weed, Justice Clarence Thomas began his vigorous dissent as follows: "Respondents Diane Monson and Angel Raich use marijuana that has never been bought or sold, that has never crossed state lines, and that has had no demonstrable effect on the national market for marijuana. If Congress can regulate this under the Commerce Clause, then it can regulate virtually anything—and the Federal government is no longer one of limited and enumerated powers."

Justice Thomas was not so blinded by a fear of weed as to obscure the constitutional approach that he and Justice Scalia had traditionally supported together.

By 2021, the federal government was no longer locking up drinkers of locally legal weed tea. In fact, federal law by this point explicitly discouraged enforcement of the federal weed ban in states with legal weed. Nevertheless, the Feds were denying legal weed growers access to banking services and were enforcing punitive tax laws designed for Mafia gangs against state-licensed weed businesses. In another minority view, Justice Thomas again castigated his colleagues for refusing to consider the wonderfully named weed case *Standing Akimbo, LLC. et al. v. United States* (2021).

Thomas started with a bit of sarcasm: "An ordinary person might think that the Federal government has retreated from its once-absolute ban on marijuana." Thomas then explained that the Feds, despite allowing legal weed to operate in most of the country, were denying access to banking services and applying tax laws designed for gangsters to licensed legal weed businesses. "As petitioners [Standing Akimbo] recently discovered," he wrote, "legality under state law and the absence of federal criminal enforcement do not ensure equal treatment."

Justice Thomas argued that the Supreme Court should have heard *Standing Akimbo* and settled the issue. But once again, a cabal of anti-weed conservative justices and big-government liberal justices agreed with each other and disagreed with him.

illegal goods such as weed. As a result, all of the states that have legalized adult-use or medical weed have passed laws pertaining only to in-state commerce. Although the U.S. Department of Justice (DOJ), in recent years, has increasingly refrained from prosecuting in-state weed sales that are legal under state law, federal prosecutors are still actively enforcing laws against interstate shipping.

For as long as interstate weed commerce remains illegal, producers in states where legal weed is relatively expensive because of high regulatory costs and high taxes are at least partially protected. In Massachusetts, for example, where the average price of bulk weed at the farm was about $3,500 per pound in 2021, local legal weed does not have to compete with supply from states where legal weed is relatively cheap, such as Washington, where state regulations and taxation are less costly and the average price of bulk weed at the farm was about $1,150 per pound in 2021.

When legal U.S. interstate commerce in weed eventually opens which could even happen before full federal legalization—cultivators and wholesalers in high-cost states like Massachusetts will have to compete with weed imported from states like Washington. The opening of interstate commerce could deal a severe blow to weed producers in states where it is expensive to produce weed because of natural conditions and input costs, or because of cannabis regulations and taxes.

California has long been the dominant force in the U.S. illegal weed market, producing (according to many estimates) more than half of America's illegal supply. California weed producers also support the country's largest legal market. In the past, much of California weed was grown outdoors. With outdoor-grown weed, as with wine, California's favorable growing climate has contributed to its comparative advantage. Many observers have naturally assumed that California will be a strong player in a future interstate weed market.

Not so fast. Let's take this step by step.

In many places, including California, efficient large-scale legal weed production has tended to move into indoor or covered spaces with some artificial lighting, including greenhouses with supplemental lighting, where crops can be harvested multiple times per year. With greenhouse production, outdoor climate is much less relevant to costs and yields. As a testament to this point, greenhouse-grown, high-quality tomatoes from British Columbia, which has little sunlight but cheap hydropower, are imported into California, while California grows acres and acres of cheap tomatoes for tomato paste. With indoor production, climate is irrelevant, except as it may affect utility costs. In a production world dominated by greenhouses,

California's climate advantage may be almost irrelevant in the future weed market.

At the same time, illegal weed in California has a relevant advantage: many square miles of rugged and inaccessible places like the national forests of the North Coast, where outdoor illegal weed growers could operate off the grid for years on end in reasonably hospitable conditions.

Indoor and greenhouse weed production are electricity-heavy, and compared with other states California has the highest commercial electricity rates outside of Hawaii. California regulations, though they may be justifiable from the point of view of social aims, do not come cheap for indoor farm producers or processors. State and local taxes and regulations governing minimum wage and other employment terms, worker safety, water rights, and environmental standards are more costly in California than they are in most other U.S. agricultural states, in Canadian provinces, or in all of Mexico. So, as we documented in Chapter 4, in California, more than in many other states, legal weed is particularly expensive relative to illegal weed.

These between-states differences in government policy and enforcement will create regulatory arbitrage opportunities for production of legal weed grown in states with less costly regulations. Industry-friendly laws, regulations, and enforcement have become a vital part of comparative advantage, just like sunshine or good roads. This is a lesson from many other farm and food industries, from eggs to milk. Unless climate is king, production will move.

The economic beneficiaries of the opening of interstate commerce will likely be producers in states with low production and processing costs, including costs of complying with regulations and taxes. The losers will be producers that attempt to remain in states with higher production and processing costs, including costs of complying with regulations. The California and Massachusetts legal weed industries may have a tough time under interstate competition.

The below-average retail weed prices in thinly populated states where business costs are low, such as Oklahoma, and in states with long-running legal weed industries and relatively light regulations, such as Colorado and Washington, suggest that both of these types of states could become net exporters of legal weed in an interstate market.

Our best assessment is that weed is not really like almonds, lettuce, or wine grapes, which are crucially dependent on climate, soil, or related conditions for yields and quality. Producing weed is more like producing eggs. Egg production is confined, and general business costs—especially chicken feed prices, but including regulations—affect location more than specific weather or soil conditions.

On the demand side, it is not yet clear whether many weed consumers are, or ever will be, particularly loyal to weed that comes from one region versus another. Increasingly, high-end weed flower is grown indoors. Even higher prices are paid for luxury processed weed products, such as vape cartridges, for which the manufacturing processes (and packaging) count for much more than where the weed was grown.

There are two main economic implications of interstate (and international) competition in legal weed markets:

(1) Expect legal farm production and processing to move to where it can be done most efficiently, given the most important input costs of energy and labor, and given the degree to which regulations affect business costs. With an open national market, trans-

port costs for weed will be a tiny share of retail prices. So weed will be grown where farm costs are low, processed where those costs are low, and consumed wherever the buyers want their weed. However, this natural trade pattern may be mitigated to some extent if California or other places impose trade-related taxes, or costly and unique testing or regulatory standards, that raise relative costs for out-of-state products trying to enter the local market.

(2) As weed production and processing settle in the best places, costs will fall, and prices in all states will converge to prices in the cheaper states. Such arbitrage-based price declines can happen very rapidly when trade restrictions are lifted. Currently there is wide variation in state-by-state wholesale weed prices, as we showed in Chapter 4. Prices are 70 percent higher in California than in Colorado, even though the California industry claims great local climate and expertise.

Finally, there's the international market, which may be the hardest thing of all to predict. Depending on how it is implemented, legal interstate trade in the U.S. could also mean legal international trade in weed by 2050, at least with some countries. Then U.S. producers compete with supply coming from places like Saskatchewan—which has a big share of the North American industrial hemp market—or, maybe even more threateningly, Mexico, where retail illegal weed from street dealers commonly sells in local markets for less than $15 per ounce! Maybe some U.S. producers will be able to compete well in a pan–North American market, or maybe not.

Meanwhile, on the top shelf, premium California weed might have to compete with premium Dutch weed. International trade in weed, like international trade in cherry tomatoes, will benefit consumers with more variety and lower prices, perhaps at a cost to some U.S. producers who must compete with imported goods. It is not obvious that U.S. weed would win in the low-price or high-quality competition, but it is also not obvious that they would not. Open markets are good at sorting out such questions.

More locally, even without global trade, local retailers are likely to find themselves competing with interstate multiproduct retail chains. The current limitations of, and implications of, state laws mean that weed retailers must specialize in weed and sell few other things. Generalized pharmacies, convenience stores, and supermarkets do not sell weed. This could easily change in the future. If Walgreens, Walmart, and Costco are competing for retail weed sales, then the local weed retailer will need to find a way to offer something unique and may be no more likely to stay in business than the local wine store.

Expected Long-Run Change #3: More Efficient Weed Farm Production and Processing Technology and Practices

The third change that we expect will drive the evolution of the legal weed industry between now and 2050 is not a regulatory change but rather a structural one: the development of new technology and practices that makes weed growing, harvesting, trimming, packaging, and distribution far more efficient than they have been until now.

The future of technological developments and their adoption is always hard to define or predict. So we don't dwell on specifics other than to point out that even in the absence of major regulatory changes, prices would still be likely to fall substantially as innovative technology and farm practices spread through the industry.

Nationwide, the weed industry is still transitioning out of a long cottage-industry phase during which high margins and legal risks incentivized costly, small-scale production over lower-cost, large-scale production. As far back as 2010, scholars such as RAND researcher Jonathan Caulkins pointed out that there is no fundamental barrier to stop weed from being produced much more cheaply and sold for orders of magnitude lower than prevailing prices.

We tend to concur. Even outdoor production takes trivial amounts of farmland and can locate where it is best suited. Greenhouse and warehouse production does not depend on climate and will move to where purchased inputs and labor are cheap. None of the inputs used for weed are inherently scarce, and skills and experience are expanding rapidly.

Going down the list: land is an almost negligible share of the cost of production; there are no major barriers to training a highly skilled weed labor force; and there is nothing especially costly about breeding or producing high-yield and high-quality seeds or seedlings. New, more efficient lighting and indoor spaces, labor-saving equipment, and new manufacturing facilities are on the horizon. In all, there is no obvious reason why the wholesale price of weed could not someday fall to $75 per pound or even $30 per pound, as Caulkins suggests. Improvements in the supply chain would push retail product prices down—at least for standard products bought by normal weed consumers.

Even below $100 per pound, weed will still be handled with care, not harvested by sloppy machines as in the case of $50-per-ton processing tomatoes, where some of the crop is simply left in the field and numerous harvested green tomatoes must be discarded at the factory. That crop is harvested by machine because it is simply not worth the labor cost of being more careful.

Remember, $100-per-pound weed still has 20 times the wholesale value of high-priced Cabernet Sauvignon grapes from Napa Valley, and nobody leaves those on the vine or on the ground. "Handle with care" will still prevail even as the price of legal weed falls in the future. We may get to routine machine trimming for routine cannabis, and we may get to precision machine harvesting for the best indoor weed that is planted to allow machines to waste less weed than hand harvesting. Innovation will come. No one knows exactly which segments or players will be winners.

But in terms of costs, weed today is still in the prehybrid phase of crop production. Biological innovation allowed corn yields to rise from 50 bushels per acre to 200 bushels per acre on the same land, while mechanical technology cut labor use to almost nothing. For weed, no one currently cares much about yield per acre, since the price is so high as to render land input costs trivial. But the same principle that applies to wine grapes or corn will eventually apply to weed. Revenue per unit of labor and unit of greenhouse electricity may be ratios that matter more. Science and engineering have only just begun to be applied in a serious way. For example, modern plant breeding and the new genetic revolution (see the 2020 Nobel Prize in Chemistry) are nowhere to be seen in weed.

Of course, no one should expect to see the same technology in weed that applies to field crops or even fruit and vegetable crops. But just as technology is a big deal in improving organic raspberries or blackberries, we may soon see a revolution in greenhouse-grown weed with, for example, more efficient lighting. Optimal humidity control and disease-resistant varieties are being studied. This revolution is increasing the ratio of dried flowers to total biomass to get high-potency flowers (and increased THC generally) at a lower cost. As with many other crops from alfalfa to carrots, quality improvements that pack more value into each unit may be more important than simply more quantity. The labor-saving innovation of mechanical trimming is not yet commonplace in the industry, but someday it will be. All of these innovations, when they happen, will lower costs per unit of the characteristics that consumers of the future care about most.

The first decade of full legalization will be a time when weed catches up to other parts of farming and agribusiness technology. After that, incentives for new and weed-specific technology will become more important.

Expected Long-Run Change #4: Real Agribusiness

Old hippies (or even young hippies) are not necessarily naturals at running agribusinesses, or at running any legal business at scale. In states with recreational legalization, we're already seeing the entry of more suits, or at least khakis and plaid shirts with typical farm and business backgrounds.

But farming itself requires a unique bundle of skills not found in the typical business background. Fund managers and private equity hustlers looking for quick returns usually don't bring much agribusiness experience to the table, and they invest in sophisticated farming schemes at their own peril.

Harvard University, after being taken to the cleaners on land and water by local yokels from San Luis Obispo to Mato Grosso, recently pulled out of big investments in orchards, vineyards, cotton, and dairy farms. In California, starting in 2012, Harvard had made large investments in land it purchased to convert to vineyards and in the irrigation water that the conversion required. Harvard finally sold the land at a major loss in 2020. Nothing raises farm costs more than suits from Wall Street trying to satisfy stock analysts looking at quarterly returns (especially for crops harvested annually).

Farm families typically have huge amounts of equity relative to their debt, and little of their money or expertise has gone into weed because of the illegality taint. So fully legal weed will attract the people who really know their ~~shit~~ fertilizer to get into the weed business big time. Once weed becomes just another agricultural commodity, you can expect the management expertise of real farmers doing real farming to kick in. And there are plenty of farm families with a cousin Louise (MBA, Wharton), and nephew Louie (engineering, Georgia Tech) in the business, along with Aunt Luisa, who is a plant science graduate from UC Davis. Modern and successful farms have a combination of technical expertise to be at the profitable edge of technology while having the financial and practical experience to understand what is likely to pay off in the field (or the greenhouse).

So far, both the Ziploc bag of mom-and-pop legal weed and the flashy legal weed in the glass jar with the dot-com logo have been grown, processed, distributed, and marketed outside regular agribusiness channels. But wait until companies similar to Driscoll's Berries (packing in retail packages in the field) are farming weed. These farming companies will work with marketers similar to Walmart or Costco to get weed to customers in a form and at a price that customers demand. Costs will be a fraction of what they are in the current 19th-century system.

But if you're into craft products, don't worry: craft weed will thrive too, if not to the extent hoped for by Ryan Stoa in his romantically optimistic 2018 book *Craft Weed*. Just as many of us enjoy driving out to a farm and picking apples one Saturday a year, or are happy to pay triple for a locally produced jelly we are told is made by somebody's grandmother, there will still be a market for those of us who want to pay more for less because it seems like fun. But competition from companies with efficient scale and modern technology will drive low-end to middle-of-the-road prices down by an order of magnitude.

To summarize: in all competitive industries, the market price is determined by the highest-cost producers that can remain in business. (Those with costs even higher than that price lose money and exit.) Low-cost producers make substantial profits, which stimulates them to expand. Those profits also stimulate observant neighbors, and new entrants, to copy what those with profits have done, and the price falls. Some businesses fail, and the efficient producers have incentives to innovate in order to harvest greater profits. The price falls again, and the cycle of innovation continues. This is the set of incentives driving the future of weed. In many ways this is an optimistic story, so does that mean huge revenues for the legal weed industry?

Are Typical Industry Futurists (and Publicists) Right about the Economic Future of Legal Weed?

In a word, no. We think many prognosticators are overestimating the total revenue in the future weed market by a mile or two! Let's explore the story and the numbers in more detail.

We should say at the outset that a wild prediction with lots of zeros in the number following a dollar sign is a way to generate enthusiasm and headlines. Carefully working through the economic fundamentals and getting less thrilling numbers may seem like a bummer. But here goes: we think that a lot of the estimates, like a $100 billion North American retail weed market in 2030, are based on a few implicit assumptions that are just far out, man.

They are far out because they have not been appropriately thought out. Economic forecasting by just arithmetic, rather than by attention to some fundamentals (followed by some arithmetic), will go wrong almost every time.

Rather than boring you by calling out every industry analyst we think is wrong, we will simply take you through the far-out logic and simple arithmetic that we think a herd of enthusiastic analysts are making in order to get to $80 billion or $100 billion or $150 billion in 2030. Then, any time you encounter such projections about the size of the legal weed market, you can ask yourself whether these kinds of far-out assumptions could be clouding someone's vision.

Here is how we think their arithmetic works. First, they start with a current retail market size. We will illustrate with some simplified but plausible numbers that are in the range of 2022 estimates. Let's say they estimate the 2022 market size (total U.S. retail sales) at about $20 billion. This is not off the wall—on the contrary, it comes mostly from officially reported state tax data.

Next, they estimate the average market price. Let's say they pick $40 per ⅛ ounce of weed, or somewhere in the neighborhood of $5,000 per pound. (Multiply $40 times 16 ounces per pound times 8 eighths per ounce to get $5,120.) To keep things simple, we stick to very round numbers. So the $20 billion in retail sales is generated by the retail quantity of 4 million pounds of weed.

Next they notice that the current $20 billion in sales is coming from only 12 states that have legalized recreational weed. Some states have medical weed, and many states still have no legal retail market to speak of. And even the states that have recreational weed are just getting started and haven't reached their full potential (in spite of Oklahoma's medical weed example). So forecasters predict, for no obvious or well-explained reason, that the market will grow by five times by 2030, from 4 million pounds to 20 million pounds. Okay, fine, but as a final necessary step they assume the price stays at $5,000 per pound. Now it's just arithmetic: 20 million pounds times $5,000 per pound equals $100 billion. Bingo.

Another type of reasoning might go like this: the legal weed market revenue grew by 30 percent last year. The forecaster might then claim to be "conservative" in applying a 25 percent compound annual growth rate (CAGR) for eight years, which gets us from $20 billion in 2022 to $120 billion by 2030. Q.E.D.

The idea that the current legal weed market *by volume* (quantity of weed produced) might only be one-fifth the size of the potential legalized U.S. market in 2030 is a bit heroic, but it's not totally implausible. It's certainly within a reasonable range that Americans could someday consume 20 million pounds a year of legal weed. That much weed (including the illegal weed) consumption might dovetail well with the automation of the labor force (including book authors and economists), as long as we have machines, including those that do economics and write books, and machines that can monitor and repair those machines.

The big problem with the simple arithmetic in the huge revenue forecasts for our future year of 2050 is that the price is very unlikely to remain constant. The big weed quantities are multiplied by a high weed price of $5,000 per pound, based on the far-out assumption that the retail price of weed will remain stable (or track inflation, if the $100 billion is in inflation-adjusted terms) even while legal weed quantities go through the roof.

But what about the market size *by total retail revenue*? Just a little data and the ideas of supply and demand tell us that over the time horizon for the quantity growth, costs of production and distribution through retail will almost surely fall (a lot). Prices cannot stay above costs, because that would make it too easy for even fools like us to be rich. For prices to remain high, costs must remain high. Will costs remain high in the legal weed market over the next three decades?

No way, dude. Fancy tea sells for $10 per pound, dried organic parsley is $20 per pound. Weed doesn't cost that much more to grow, manufacture, or package than fancy tea or organic parsley. Unless there is some specialized limiting resource (like fancy terroir), competition, economies of scale, technology, consolidation, and other efficiencies bring down the costs rapidly as markets develop—even if taxes and regulations remain costly.

The current prices and costs of weed are simply not sustainable. Prices fall when efficiency and interstate trade bring down costs all along the supply chain, from growing to testing to retailing. Modern farming has not yet transformed weed as it has transformed crops from almonds and alfalfa to walnuts and zucchini. Amazon and Costco could bring down distribution and retailer costs even in the premium segment.

To sum up the few pages above in five words:
Prices will fall. Be ready.

California in 2050

To illustrate the points in this chapter (a bit) more concretely, let's zoom in on the future of legal weed to 2050 in our home state of California, where we have the most empirical basis for making not-so-wild speculations. On the basis of the current state of the California market and the four long-run changes discussed earlier in this chapter, we make some predictions about regulatory changes and some conservative projections about how California weed prices and market sizes could move between 2022 and 2050.

We use rough estimates and round numbers to emphasize that even current numbers are not known with much precision. But our starting points are within a plausible range based on the best data we have seen. You can see all of them in Table 6. All the dollar figures are adjusted for any inflation to represent 2022 dollars.

We start with 2022 California weed prices of about $800 per pound at the farm, $2,000 per pound at wholesale (delivered to the retailer), and $4,000 per pound at retail. (Note that these prices take into account rapidly falling California farm prices for weed in late 2021. Some of our earlier tables, figures, and charts use previous years' higher prices as starting points.)

Next, we consider the fact that 2022 low-end retail prices in California are more than double the low-end prices in Washington State ($3 per gram for ounces of low-end flower). Such large dispersion in prices between two states in the same region is possible because arbitrage is illegal: that is, current restrictions in trade keep Washington State weed products out of the California market. But history and common economic sense tell us that those kinds of price differences will not survive interstate commerce.

There is no other crop whose prices for the same product (absent huge differences in the characteristics of the product itself) vary as much as outdoor weed prices do across America. There is

TABLE 6. Speculative estimates for California's legal weed market in 2020, 2035, and 2050 (numbers in 2022 U.S. dollars, rounded to the nearest $10)

Regulatory assumptions	2022	2035	2050
Status of weed under federal law	Illegal	Decriminalized	Regulated
Status of weed sales under state law[a]	Mostly legal in about 25 states	Legal in 40 states	Legal in all 50 states
Interstate shipping of weed	Illegal	Legal	Legal
Weed-specific taxes	State, local	State, local	Federal, state, local

Alternative farm price estimates	2022	2035	2050
Avg farm price range, 1 lb raw flower (range)	$200 to $2,500	$50 to $2,000	$20 to $1,500
Avg farm price, 1 lb raw flower	$800	$300	$100

Alternative Distributor price estimates	2022	2035	2050
Avg distributor price range, 1 lb packaged weed (range across all forms including flower, oil, edibles, etc.)	$400 to $5,000	$70 to $4,000	$30 to $3,000
Avg distributor price, 1 lb packaged weed	$2,000	$600	$180
Avg distributor markup over farm price	150%	100%	80%

Retail price estimates (before tax)	2022	2035	2050
Avg retail price range, 1 lb packaged weed (range across all forms)	$2,000 to $15,000	$500 to $15,000	$100 to $15,000
Avg retail price, 1 lb packaged weed	$4,000	$1,050	$300
Avg retail markup over distributor price (including all taxes)	100%	75%	67%

Retail market size estimate (before tax)	2022	2035	2050
Total retail revenue	$5.0 billion	$2.1 billion	$750 million

[a] In 2022 there is huge variation across states, especially for medical-only states. In some states like Oklahoma, weed is readily available and the medical distinction is a modest distraction for most sellers and buyers (except out-of-state buyers, who are excluded from the legal market). But in other states like New York, strict and exclusionary medical rules limit the market to a very small number of legal buyers and sellers.

also no clear reason that costs would be lower in Washington State unless the differences were based on regulations. Cost of production for other crops where markets are integrated—such as wine grapes, apples, and blueberries—are all similar between states.

This tells us that when state-by-state restrictions are lifted, prices at the farm will fall and farm production will move to the most efficient regions. For example, indoor production may abandon California, which has high electricity prices. Moreover, weed is not yet grown with modern management and technology at scale, and modern weed biology is in its infancy.

With modern efficiencies and scale (Figure 28), the average farm price of weed could fall to $300 per pound, $200 per pound, or lower. Already in 2021, the lowest end of farm prices in Washington is $300 or lower. We also expect markups between farm and distributor, and between distributor and retailer, to fall from their current levels (maybe 80–120 percent) to lower levels (maybe 50–60 percent), bringing legal weed more into line with other agricultural industries. In the most extreme example shown in Table 6, the retail price of the processed and packaged product falls to $300 per pound (not including taxes)—less than 10 percent of the price in the current California market.

Even if, as we assume in Table 6, the volume (number of pounds) of legal weed sold approximately doubles over time, the effect of the rising volume on total retail market size will be overwhelmed by the effect of more steeply falling prices, and the end result will be an industry much *smaller* in revenue terms than the current legal weed market. In our example, the California retail market size falls by four-fifths between 2022 and 2050, from $5 billion to $750 million.

FIGURE 28. Extraction at MJBizCon. Credit: Robin Goldstein.

To Those in the Business: Do Not Despair

We warned you earlier that economists were dismal. But when Thomas Carlyle called Thomas Malthus "dismal" 200 years ago, it was because Malthus did not see how farm prices could fall. Carlyle did not think Malthus was wrong, just dismal for talking about it.

We take the opposite position to Malthus's. We see good news for consumers and perfectly reasonable (and normal) times for good farmers and well-run agribusinesses that process and market weed. What we do not see is wildly high times for speculators (except perhaps for those who speculate in technology and guess precisely right about which technologies and which companies will win).

A surprising result of these projections (at least to us) is that when prices fall enough, then the market—measured by revenue, not quantity—must shrink to a small fraction of its current size by value, even when it doubles by volume. This would throw a serious wrench into the projections of lots of industry analysts and even more investor publicists.

Our projections for weed are in line with the trend in relative prices of food and farm products, from the era before innovation to the current era, after many innovations have had their major influence. From alfalfa to zucchini, farm and food prices declined substantially as innovation was applied to agriculture and agribusiness.

But maybe we are wrong about the total market revenue shrinking. Revenue could stay more constant or even grow, especially if regulations became more costly, or if innovations were blocked by regulations, or if taxes that were included in market prices rose enough. But we see no way that legal weed revenue would grow by a factor of 8 or 10 or 15 even in such an odd scenario. Prices could also remain higher than we think, for longer than we think, for reasons we cannot foresee. However, even if the total retail market winds up growing modestly, we still think that sky-high projections about the overall size of the weed pie appear to come from somebody with a serious case of the munchies.

So What?

Why should you care that many projections are wrong? Let's sum up the implications of the effects we have described above and leave you with five concrete takeaways about the legal weed market in 2050:

1. Quantity goes up.
2. Production and processing move.
3. Weed, both legal and illegal, gets cheaper.
4. Total retail revenue might fall, maybe by a lot—not rise by an order of magnitude.
5. Don't tell the suits!

We now summarize each of these takeaways.

1. Quantity Goes Up

All indications are for steady growth in the quantity (by weight) of legal weed production, supply, and consumption in North America measured by the pounds of weed used in production of the products sold. So, if you want to measure the size of the industry by pounds of weed produced and consumed, it is growing bigger and will continue to do so. We see gradual increases in per capita legal consumption in regions with legal weed now, as the product reaches more diverse consumer groups and as the legal weed "pie" expands by volume. We are optimistic that regulations will gradually be adjusted to better match market realities.

Assume average per capita consumption of legal weed doubles in 30 years in places that have legal access to weed. Full legalization in the U.S., Canada, and perhaps Mexico would more than double the number of consumers with local access to legal weed. So, total quantity of legal weed could go up by 400 percent. Pretty impressive. This would mean that the North American legal weed quantity could grow in round terms from 7.5 million pounds to 30 million pounds. (Notice that we do not predict the demise of illegal weed, which we think may shrink but will still hold its own by adopting its own innovations.)

2. *Production and Processing Move*

The question of where legal weed production and processing occur is another matter, and we are not predicting the specific states or counties to which they will migrate. That is part of the point. No one can really know where yet, because lots about regional comparative advantage is still shaking out. But the underlying forces of comparative advantage will drive the where, and it will be different from the current geographical distribution of production and processing, which is fragmented by state borders and controlled in part by state-by-state regulators.

States like Oklahoma, with lower labor costs, utility costs, and regulatory costs, will be the most predictable winners in terms of attracting production and processing. But they may face tough competition from Idaho, South Dakota, Alberta, or Sonora.

3. *Weed Gets Cheaper*

All the data and modeling we have seen suggests that costs of weed production, processing, distribution, and retailing will fall hugely in the next 30 years. Let's repeat some conservative example numbers to cement the implications. A pound of standard weed that is now priced at $800 per pound leaving a farm might fall to $100. Given declines in marketing margins, weed whose retail price is currently $30 to $50 in most U.S. states could end up with a retail price of $2 to $3 per eighth.

4. Total Retail Revenue Will Likely Fall, and Maybe by a Lot—Not Rise by an Order of Magnitude

Nobody in any business *really* cares about quantity by volume. What people care about is the money, and there is a lot less room for big profit growth if total revenue falls. Total retail revenue (not including taxes, unless you are the tax man)—pretax retail price times retail quantity—determines how much the different industry links in the value chain have to share. (Recall that in a supply chain one company's cost is another company's revenue.) Each link in the chain generates its own value that determines the revenue share of that link. Each company has incentives around the net revenue, but the gross total retail revenue is the amount of money in the system and is a reasonable measure of size of the whole weed value chain.

Let's say that we start with a current total U.S. industry of 2.5 million pounds (dried flower equivalent) at about $4,000 per pound, or about $10 billion at retail. Assume that the U.S. quantity rises hugely, by 10 times (meeting or exceeding optimistic predictions about growth in consumer use and expansion to new geographical areas), to 25 million pounds of legal retail weed quantity. Meanwhile, the average U.S. retail price falls to $300 per pound. The result is retail revenue of $7.5 billion. Bottom line: the legal weed business is not hugely bigger but instead smaller than the business in 2020!

5. Don't Tell the Suits!

Could we be wrong? Sure, but how wrong? Let's imagine that the U.S. quantity of legal weed goes up by 12.5 times, to 50 million pounds. That's a lot of stoned Americans, but maybe there's a 10-year pandemic. And let's also imagine that, for whatever reasons, legal weed totally wipes out illegal weed, and illegal weed can't compete anymore. This probably wouldn't be an enforcement effect. With weed already everywhere, nobody expects the U.S. government to make a sudden U-turn and out-Nixon Nixon, jailing old hippies and storming poor neighborhoods over weed again. But if legal prices fall fast enough, we could see illegal weed fade away much as illegal liquor and wine have faded away.

So imagine that almost all weed is legal weed, and there's 50 million pounds of it consumed every year, and the retail price falls to $300 per pound. Multiply 50 million times $300 and you get $15 billion: only 1.5 times the legal retail market size we started with, not the 5x or 10x growth everyone is talking about. And that is the best we can do!

There might just not be enough money to keep today's breed of suits interested. They'd best go back to pumping WeWork or Theranos stock.

8   *How to Survive Legalization*

What can a legal weed business in North America do with all the information we've dumped on you in the previous seven chapters? How do you survive to 2030, 2040, or 2050 if you're a legal weed entrepreneur, operator, or investor?

Before answering, we begin with one more looming question.

Will National Legalization Help U.S. Weed Businesses?

U.S. national legalization and the opening of interstate commerce might not help many of today's legal weed businesses in the United States. National legalization will help some farm and manufacturing businesses in some states and will terminate others. In many states, opening a national market would eliminate most legal weed production because, like other farm production, weed will probably be concentrated in the regions where it is best suited to be grown from a cost and climate perspective.

Part of the answer to any question about changing national rules depends on details of federal regulation. Federal regulations and taxes could present additional problems for businesses that previously had to answer only to the state. A national U.S. weed market with interstate trade could take many different shapes. The federal government could legalize weed without regulating it and could allow states to opt out of weed legalization, just as California had almost no regulations of medical weed for two decades and then allowed counties to opt out of weed legalization. A situation like this could potentially continue for a decade or more.

However U.S. national legalization is implemented, some weed businesses in some states will win, and many others will lose. In the competitive market of 2050, outcomes will depend on cost comparisons on the low end and on consumer perceptions on the high end.

In a market with interstate commerce, comparative advantage will determine where weed is grown and processed. No one yet really knows what a technically sophisticated weed industry will demand from the local environment, but it would be odd if Humboldt County or the state of Massachusetts turned out to be especially well suited for this crop when they are not suited for any other crop. Just as Kansas grows wheat, California grows lettuce, and Iowa grows hogs, the best-suited regions for growing with scale economies, efficient farming and processing, and low labor, electricity, and manufacturing costs are likely to capture the low end of the U.S. weed market. Recall that we discussed above that climate and soil may be less important for the future location for weed than electricity and labor costs. Just as no one would choose San Francisco or Boston to locate a manufacturing company that depends on low-wage labor, weed will go to where its inputs are competitively priced.

What will weed producers and processors do to remain competitive in states whose regulations (e.g., pesticide testing) or electricity are more costly than other states' regulations? Can California and Massachusetts compete on price with cheap legal weed from

Washington State (currently as low as $300 per pound for legal out-door-grown weed, versus $1,000 per pound in California or $3,000 per pound in Massachusetts)?

What Strategies Will Help Businesses Survive in the Long Run?

Next, we try to usefully apply our observations on competitiveness by discussing four potential survival strategies that could help weed producers and processors survive even in some of the scariest scenarios described above:

1. Get your government to impose local standards on weed from out of state.
2. Develop regions that make claims as premium places of origin for weed.
3. Create a following for local weed that allows for price premiums compared to out-of-state weed.
4. Raise awareness that weed shipped into your state may not meet local standards.

These strategies apply to production and processing of weed. Wholesale and retail businesses will be where the customers are, and that has little to do with where the weed comes from. People in Boston get guacamole just like people in L.A., even though the avocados are from 3,000 miles away. The fancy wine culture of New York City has much more to do with wine from Bordeaux and Napa than it has to do with the Finger Lakes District upstate. Likewise, there will be weed retailers in L.A. even if the weed is mostly grown in a field outside Tulsa.

In our discussion of these strategies, we use California as an example, but the survival strategies we discuss apply to many legal weed states.

Survival Strategy #1: Impose Local Standards on Out-of-State Imports

To counteract cheap weed importation from out of state, individual states could pass legislation that prohibits the in-state sale of weed imported from states whose safety (or environmental) regulations are less restrictive (and thus less costly) than their own state's regulations. It is unclear whether such legislation, if enacted, would withstand U.S. Constitutional Commerce Clause scrutiny.

In a somewhat analogous situation, for instance, California set animal-welfare standards for eggs imported into California that exceeded national minimum standards, and such standards seem to pass constitutional muster. However, domestic egg producers must still compete with out-of-state producers whose products meet California standards but whose costs of producing eggs are otherwise lower.

One common trick used in international trade is to get your local politicians to create local standards that are cheaper for local growers to meet. For example, a state could ban traceable amounts of some pesticide that is not used locally. Or a state could require meeting some labor regulatory standard for weed shipped in that is already required for local weed companies.

Similarly for weed, some states are likely to have comparative cost-of-production advantages over others. These advantages may derive from many factors besides regulatory costs, such as electricity, labor, or environmental compliance costs.

Survival Strategy #2: Develop Individual Regions as
Premium Places of Origin for Weed

One way that high-cost weed producers in expensive regions can compete successfully with low-cost producers is to convince buyers that their higher weed prices are justified by premium or "super-premium" quality. In the premium weed market, margins are higher, costs of farm production are a smaller component of total costs, and consumers may derive extra value from labels marketed on the basis of their place of origin.

California's long-standing reputation for quality weed labor and management (and its long and rich history of legal and illegal production) may provide some authenticity to these claims. If consumers already have the perception that California is a prestigious origin for weed, then they may be willing to pay a premium for weed from California, as they are willing to do for some appellations of origin for wine. But the high-end market, however it is defined, likely represents only a fraction of the overall weed market.

Of course, weed can be most easily marketed on the basis of its origin if it is outdoor-grown. However, outdoor-grown cannabis is now often the cheapest and least potent form of weed. This is in part a legacy of illegal weed, when growers avoided aerial detection by shading weed with other canopies. Weed grown in the shade tends to be less potent; thus an association between outdoor-grown weed and weaker weed arose.

Despite the lower potency of outdoor-grown weed, some consumers and medical practitioners prefer outdoor-grown weed for its fuller spectrum of cannabinoids or its milder effects. That could create a niche market for high-priced outdoor appellations.

Survival Strategy #3: Create a Following for Local Weed That Allows Price Premiums Compared to Weed That Is Shipped in from Other States or Countries

This strategy is useful only for regions with lots of local consumers who can be convinced to buy local even if there is no government-imposed interstate trade barrier or official appellation with claims of high quality.

Local food enthusiasts like supporting food businesses. Some die-hards go to extremes of eating only local food, even if that means no vegetables but sauerkraut and pickles for half the year. Local weed buyers may not need to go to such extremes to buy and consume locally—they may just have to pay higher prices for lower-quality products.

Local weed farms and manufacturing companies develop a following together with local retailers. Promotions with real local farmers and workers foster a sense of community. Just about everyone wants to support their friends and neighbors. Cultivating that sense of community is costly, and a marketing effort may not pay unless businesses in the local weed industry work together and have the support of local government and retailers. Locals may sell best where there is a legacy industry with a history. If you're from Oakland, Cleveland weed may be a harder sell than keeping the hippie tradition alive by buying the weed produced by your barber's brother-in-law who is just trying to keep the 40-year old business afloat.

Can "local" as a product attribute be more than a niche in major retail markets? Maybe not, but it may be the survival niche for some heritage businesses.

Survival Strategy #4: Raise Awareness That Weed Shipped into Your State May Not Meet Local Standards

If you can't get people to want your product, then denigrate your competitor's product. A time-honored practice in international trade is to try to block entry of imports by whatever means necessary. That was Survival Strategy #1. But if that fails, a backup plan is to require origin labeling. Even if consumers cannot be convinced that the local weed is better, they may be convinced that the imports are sub-par, especially on health, safety, or environmental grounds. The key is to focus on attributes that the buyers cannot easily check or monitor.

Most of us think our local area is a pretty good place to be, especially if we have standards for safety, high wages, or environmental quality. Pointing out that weed shipped in may not meet some local regulations could help boost and maintain the local customer base for local products. This strategy does not work for the bulk of buyers who are just looking for a bargain, but it may be enough to keep some of the local suppliers in business.

The First Time We Tried Weed

ROBIN:

The year was 1990. I was in the ninth grade. My friend Seth had scored some weed from an eleventh grader he knew. The time had come.

On the phone in his locked bedroom, Seth told me in hushed and wavering tones about the quality of the goods and the lengths to which he'd gone to get them, cornering goths in school parking lots, cutting back on his CD spending, and so on. I was scared, but given the circumstances, I could not turn down Seth's gift. I had to start a new life as a drug user. For the next week we nervously plotted the mission: where, when, how.

Seth was taller than me, with dark, bushy eyebrows. He didn't say much, but when he did say something, he did it with conviction. He had recently taken me to a Jello Biafra spoken-word performance at the University of Massachusetts and was a rebel with several well-articulated causes. For instance, Seth was in favor of flag burning and for a while he had considered it his civic duty to burn the American flag.

There are some things we do only because they are prohibited: actions that wouldn't even occur to us but for the fact that polite society considers them to be unacceptable. When we curse, for instance, we choose our words precisely for their offensiveness. When a formerly offensive curse stops being so offensive over time (like "damn"), we replace it with a new curse word that is more offensive. Curse words' whole force comes from their prohibition, whether official or unofficial. Similarly, the main and possibly only appeal of flag burning was the idea that it was (at least theoretically) illegal.

Seth had never actually burnt a flag until the previous week, when he and I had gone out in my backyard and done the deed together, recording it on my family's Camcorder. Once we were out there, Seth and I quickly learned that burning the flag isn't as easy as it sounds. We were ninth graders who had grown up in the highly inoffensive college town of Northampton, Massachusetts. Our parents hadn't signed us up for Boy Scouts or taken us camping very much, and it hadn't occurred to us to douse the flag in something first. So the flag kept going out, and our fingers got pretty hot. Most of the time, Seth and I were in more danger than the flag was.

We were more successful at cursing than we were at flag burning. The previous year Seth and I had formed a rap group called S.O.B. (Students of Bakunin). Our group was named after the Russian anarchist Mikhail Bakunin, who, in his magnum opus *God and the State,* wrote like a woke white Northamptonite 150 years ahead of his time: "It is the peculiarity of privilege and of every privileged position to kill the intellect and heart of man. The privileged man, whether he be privileged politically or economically, is a man depraved in intellect and heart."

Bakunin despised democracy or any other form of central social control, and so did Seth and I. Democracy was responsible for the school dress code and the rules against cursing in class, and it was responsible for George H.W. Bush's license to spend our money dropping bombs on Iraq. In S.O.B.'s recorded tracks "Iraq: Another Vietnam" and "Bush, or Is It Mussolini?," we scratched records on top of the president's words.

The heyday of S.O.B. would span most of the ninth and tenth grades, during which we released two albums under the indie anarchist record label Shitting Horse Records, a label that Seth and I also owned and operated. The marketing thrust and primary selling point of S.O.B.'s music was its level of profanity—an incredibly excessive level of profanity that would have been prohibited by any U.S. commercial record label larger than Shitting Horse Records. We sold nine copies of our album to a niche market of middle schoolers who were still learning to curse and wanted content more offensive than could be legally produced by mainstream labels.

Still, saying yes to drugs?

The U.S. government had teed it up for us as something more than just another act of adolescent rebellion. It was frying your brain. It was supporting terrorists. It was a sinister new identity, the embodiment of everything our parents wanted us not to be, even if they had smoked weed themselves in the 1960s.

I was positive that every word of this government propaganda was total bullshit. All I had to do to join the rebel alliance was take a few puffs from a joint. The only problem was that I was terrified to do it, out of a deep fear that every word of this government propaganda was entirely correct.

On the designated afternoon, just before Seth arrived, when his father was still 10 minutes away from dropping him off, I started to freak out. I opened the phone book—yes, I am almost as old as Sumner—and I looked up a drug counseling hotline. I dialed their toll-free 1–800 number from my family's landline, and a kindly-sounding lady picked up.

She said: "Hello?"

This confused me, because I noticed that she didn't say, "Hello, Drug Hotline?" She just said hello in a nice way, with a Boston accent, like my cousin Ruthie.

I stuttered a bit and then said to the lady: "Uh, is this the Drug Hotline?"

The lady seemed a little surprised to be hearing from me, but after a medium-length pause, she seemed to be on board with the program. "Sure, what's up?"

My voice was trembling. I said something like: "I am thinking of trying marijuana. Can you tell me why I shouldn't? What are the risks?"

After another long pause, she gave me a short and simple answer: "Marijuana is a mind-altering drug. An illegal, mind-altering drug."

As I was beginning to contemplate the metaphysics of this idea, the doorbell rang. I slammed down the phone and went to let in Seth. His father, who was our city's superintendent of schools, gave me a stately nod hello.

After the superintendent had driven off, Seth reached into the pocket of his hoodie and took out a Ziploc bag full of sticks, branches, and leaves. He peeled open the bag and held it out for me to smell. It was like rotten flowers, but at the same time, also a little bit like my family vacations to Lake Winnipesaukee, when I was seven or eight and my parents would hang out with the Bartolinis out on the lakeshore while I would play with their daughter Jessica inside the cabin.

Before long our other friend Julien, whom we'd also roped in, had arrived. The three of us solemnly walked out the front door and started walking toward the tracks. If there had been only two middle schoolers, maybe it wouldn't have happened. One, never. But with three boys egging each other on, we chose an area of grass and brush that was tucked in just below the tracks and became pot smokers. Seth, our intrepid leader, naturally went first.

There was a moderate and variable breeze. The fall leaves had deep colors of red and orange. Julien and I watched their dry fragments swirling around in the air as Seth said goodbye to his last few moments on earth as a non–drug user. We watched a lone Eggo Waffle half-wrapper blow across the tracks and disappear into the sky like a lost balloon.

Seth stuffed the mulch into a pipe and lit it with his older brother's Bic like it was no big deal. A modest-size puff of smoke billowed out of Seth's mouth, and within seconds he was coughing uncontrollably like a deranged madman. He passed the pipe to Julien, who had valiantly agreed to go second but was spooked by Seth's hacking. Julien waited a couple minutes for Seth to calm down, then punted with a feeble and marginally successful draw.

I was up third. Both of my hands were shaking by the time Julien passed me the pipe. At the touch of pipe to unstable left fingers, the ghost of the kindly Drug Hotline Lady appeared before me, and repeated: It's a mind-altering drug. An illegal, mind-altering drug.

What was interesting about the Drug Hotline Lady's statement was that her reasons not to do it were exactly the same as our reasons to do it. Our very purpose was to conquer the fear that the Drug Hotline Lady and her kin had drilled into every bone in our bodies, through the vast War on Drugs that had stretched through our whole adolescence.

The War on Drugs and the Drug Hotline Lady played just the roles we needed them to play in our lives. Their purpose was to be disobeyed. Illegal drugs wouldn't be illegal drugs without the fear of wigging out or getting caught. Let us not forget masochism in the list of important human motivations. Masochism solves a growing problem in our society: Where is the danger?

In 1990 as today, for many of us the world has gotten very safe. Many of the opportunities we had for behaving irresponsibly and putting ourselves at risk have faded over the past few decades. Once we strapped on armor, fought lions, and sailed into uncharted waters. Today we chase tornadoes, get tats, and take Whip-Its.

If we seek courage, we must first find fear. These days, it is not so easy to find. Fear is an integral part of the ayahuasca, base-jumping, and marriage-proposal rituals. Sometimes fear is a cost, other times a costly benefit.

What saves courage is the human penchant for unlimited innovation when it comes to generating real fear, even in the absence of real danger. In the high age of safety, we persevere, saved by our unlimited ability to find new ways of scaring ourselves, and each other, shitless.

I sucked in, and tried my best to hold it in until there was a lot of smoke in my mouth and a little bit in my lungs too, which I immediately spewed out with far greater force than the force with which it had come in. I don't think I actually got high—that would not happen for four more years—but I am at least sure that a small amount of THC entered my bloodstream. Anyway, I did better on my first time than Bill Clinton says he did.

I knew I had really done it because my nose started running, and Seth had explained to me that a runny nose was a typical side effect of weed. The only other effect I could discern was possibly the most extreme guilt of all time.

Seth's nose was running too.

I asked him if he felt anything. He said maybe.

He asked me if I felt anything. I said maybe.

DAN:

My first weed story is the more mundane experience of the previous generation, with my first year of college at the time of Woodstock. Robin talks of fear, of which I recall none. But this was also college, not middle school. In my campus culture 50 years ago, weed was routine, at least for some of us.

Even then there was a cultural divide. In San Luis Obispo, California, at the end of the sixties, it was cowboys versus hippies, and I was in the awkward position of being both—a hippie in the cattle pens and a cowboy in moccasins riding a bike.

Pretty soon, of course, even the cowboys were smoking, and growing, weed.

Conclusion

Five Pipe Dreams about Legal Weed

Finally, we leave you with five summary insights to remember us with. These insights come in the form of "pipe dreams" about legal weed that have been floating around for a while, followed by a reminder of how we hope we have shattered each in this book. (Sorry, even our bottom lines are framed as counterarguments, so it seems that we really are just dismal guys.)

The pipe dreams are as follows:

1. As more states legalize, legal weed will win and illegal weed will recede.
2. Corporate chieftains will make big profits on legal weed.
3. Sales revenue of legal weed simply must grow exponentially—because after all, it's a big market out there.
4. U.S. national legalization will help legal weed businesses.
5. Either legal weed will collapse completely because it cannot compete, or legal weed will become the government's new cash cow.

We conclude by splashing each of these pipe dreams with a big dose of cold water.

Pipe Dream #1: As More States Legalize, Legal Weed
Will Win and Illegal Weed Will Recede

We say: Under the legal and regulatory systems that now apply, legal weed may never claim the majority of North American retail sales. Consumers have shown that they are not willing to replace illegal weed with high-priced legal weed. Some consumers may not know the difference, and for most buyers illegal weed is a legitimate substitute for legal weed. In some states, laws and regulations must change before legal weed can win. Maybe national legalization will be an opportunity for more legal-friendly regulations and taxes, but maybe that is just a pipe dream.

Pipe Dream #2: Corporate Chieftains Will Make Big
Profits on Legal Weed

We say: Although corporations have been entering and will continue to enter the legal weed market, most investors in legal weed have been losing money. Yes, sooner or later, someone will time it right, buy low, sell high, and make money. Some lucky souls have already picked the right moment to buy some stock before a surge and dump their overpriced weed investments before the latest collapse. But in general, outside investors have already lost enormous amounts of money on legal weed, and we expect that unless the situation changes, many will continue to do so. Others, perhaps those waiting for clarity in a smoky environment, will simply avoid legal weed for a while. At some point, serious investment in technology and other innovation will transform the industry, but that development is more likely to be led by farmers and agribusiness than by hedge funds and MBAs.

Pipe Dream #3: Sales Revenue of Legal Weed Simply
Must Grow Exponentially—Because after All,
It's a Big Market Out There

We say: Many analysts predict that the $20 billion U.S. legal weed market must grow and that North American consumers will soon be spending $80–$100 billion on legal weed. But recent evidence, a few plausible numbers, and some simple calculations indicate that the market price of legal weed could easily fall to 15 percent of the current price, which means that even if legal quantity rises, revenue in the legal segment could fall rather than rise. Even—or especially—if all goes well, future total revenue in the North American legal retail weed market may ultimately add up to a fraction of the size many predict.

Pipe Dream #4: U.S. National Legalization Will
Help Legal Weed Businesses

We say: Some basic data plus economic reasoning indicate that U.S. national legalization of weed will help some businesses, but national legalization is likely to make competition harder for more businesses than it helps. National legalization will be especially challenging for businesses in states on the U.S. East Coast and in California, where regulations make legal weed production and marketing expensive compared with weed produced in other states. In an open North American market, the Northwest, Midwest, South, or any place with cheap energy and labor could produce the bulk of North America's legal weed. Mexico could also claim a share of the legal weed market. Many current and planned U.S. legal weed businesses may not be viable in an open North

American market. To survive, they may need a U.S. Supreme Court willing to protect them from the Commerce Clause or NAFTA.

Pipe Dream #5: Either Legal Weed Will Collapse Completely Because It Cannot Compete, or Legal Weed Will Become the Government's New Cash Cow

We say: The truth is less dramatic and more interesting. Legal weed is likely to grow gradually in quantity and may increase its market share of all weed as efficiency and better business practices cause the price to fall and put pressure on profits in the illegal segment. So, consistent with pipe dreams #3 and #4, government revenue will be a moderate supplement in many jurisdictions that learn to keep their regulatory and tax enthusiasm in check. The productivity of the cash cow depends on keeping her fit, and nothing will dry up the tax money flow faster than crippling regulations. The best way to dry up the flow of milk is to drive away the cow because the grass is greener somewhere else.

Bibliography

Ammerman, S., S. Ryan, and W. P. Adelman. (2015). "The Impact of Marijuana Policies on Youth: Clinical, Research, and Legal Update." *Pediatrics* 135(3): e769–85. Available at: https://pediatrics.aappublications.org /content/135/3/e769.

Arcview Market Research / BDS Analytics. (2020). *The State of Legal Cannabis Markets.* 7th ed. Edited by T. Adams. Available at: https://bdsa.com /wp-content/uploads/2020/01/SOLCM7_2020_Update_BDS_FR.pdf.

Armington, P. S. (1969). "A Theory of Demand for Products Distinguished by Place of Production." *Staff Papers* (International Monetary Fund) 16(1): 159–78. Available at: https://www.jstor.org/stable/3866403.

Astorino, D. M. (2019). "5 U.S. Lounges Where You Can Smoke Weed (Legally)." *AFAR,* August 16. Available at: https://www.afar.com/magazine/lounges-where-you-can-legally-smoke-weed-in-the-united-states.

Baum, D. (2016). "Legalize It All." *Harper's,* March 31. Available at: https:// harpers.org/archive/2016/04/legalize-it-all.

Becker, G. S., and K. M. Murphy. (1988). "A Theory of Rational Addiction." *Journal of Political Economy* 96(4): 675–700. Available at: https://www .jstor.org/stable/1830469.

Becker, G. S., K. M. Murphy, and M. Grossman. (2006). "The Market for Illegal Goods: The Case of Drugs." *Journal of Political Economy* 114(1): 38–60. Available at: https://doi.org/10.1086/498918.

Bennett, E. A. (2018). "Extending Ethical Consumerism Theory to Semi-legal Sectors: Insights from Recreational Cannabis." *Agriculture and Human*

Values 35(2): 295–317. Available at: https://link.springer.com/article/10
.1007/s10460-017-9822-8.

Bidwell, L.C., J.M. Ellingson, H.C. Karoly, S.L. York-Williams, L.N. Hitch-
cock, B.L. Tracy, J. Klawitter, C. Sempio, A.D. Bryan, and K.E. Hutchison.
(2020). "Association of Naturalistic Administration of Cannabis Flower
and Concentrates with Intoxication and Impairment." *JAMA Psychiatry*
77(8): 787–96. Available at: https://doi.org/10.1001/jamapsychiatry
.2020.0927.

Bohannon, J., R. Goldstein, and A. Herschkowitsch. (2010). "Can People
Distinguish Pâté from Dog Food?" *Chance* 23(2): 43–46. Available at:
https://www.researchgate.net/publication/239805135_Can_People_
Distinguish_Pate_from_Dog_Food.

Bolda, M., L. Tourte, J. Murdock, and D.A. Sumner. (2019). "Sample Costs to
Produce and Harvest Organic Strawberries." University of California
Agriculture and Natural Resources Cooperative Extension and Agricul-
tural Issues Center, UC Davis Department of Agricultural and Resource
Economics. Available at: https://ucanr.edu/sites/uccesc/files/312501.pdf.

Booth, M. (2005). *Cannabis: A History.* London: Picador.

Brown, J. (2008). "Guidelines for Security and Non-diversion of Marijuana
Grown for Medical Use." Memo from California Attorney General Jerry
Brown. Available at: https://medicalmarijuana.procon.org/wp-content
/uploads/sites/37/brown_guidelines_aug08.pdf.

Budman, K.B. (1977). "A First Report on the Impact of California's New
Marijuana Law (SB 95)." Sacramento: California State Office of Narcotics
and Drug Abuse. Available at: https://www.ojp.gov/ncjrs/virtual-library
/abstracts/impact-californias-new-marijuana-law-sb-95-report-1st.

Cadelago, C., and J. Miller. (2016). "Money and Marijuana: Donors with Ties
to Industry Give to Legalize Pot." *Sacramento Bee,* August 26. Available at:
www.sacbee.com/news/politics-government/capitol-alert/article97932817
.html.

California Department of Cannabis Control (DCC). (2021). Cannabis
Regulations. Available at: https://cannabis.ca.gov.

California Department of Tax and Fee Administration (CDTFA). (2020).
Cannabis Tax Revenues for 2018–2021. Available at: https://www.cdtfa
.ca.gov.

Cannabis Benchmarks. (2021). Premium Reports. Available at: https://
reports.cannabisbenchmarks.com.

Catapano, R., N. Buttrick, J. Widness, R. Goldstein, and L. R. Santos. (2014).
"Capuchin Monkeys Do Not Show Human-Like Pricing Effects." *Frontiers
in Decision Neuroscience* 5(1330). Available at: https://www
.frontiersin.org/articles/10.3389/fpsyg.2014.01330/full.

Caulkins, J. (2010a). "Altered State? Assessing How Marijuana Legalization in
California Could Influence Marijuana Consumption and Public Budgets."
RAND Occasional Papers OP-315. Available at: www.rand.org/content
/dam/rand/pubs/occasional_papers/2010/RAND_OP315.pdf.

Caulkins, J. (2010b). "Estimated Cost of Production for Legalized Cannabis."
RAND Working Papers WR-764. Available at: https://www.rand.org/pubs
/working_papers/WR764.html.

Caulkins, J. P., A. Hawken, B. Kilmer, M. A. R. Kleiman, K. Pfrommer, J. Jacob
Pruess, and T. Shaw. (2013). "High Tax States: Options for Gleaning
Revenue from Legal Cannabis." *Oregon Law Review* 91(4): 1041–68.
Available at: https://www.rand.org/pubs/external_publications/EP51413
.html.

Caulkins, J. P., B. Kilmer, M. A. R. Kleiman, R. MacCoun, G. Midgette,
P. Oglesby, R. Liccardo Pacula, and P. Reuter. (2015). "Options and Issues
Regarding Marijuana Legalization." *RAND Perspectives* PE-149. Available
at: www.rand.org/pubs/perspectives/PE149.html.

Choo, E. K., M. Benz, N. Zaller, O. Warren, K. L. Rising, and K. J. McConnell.
(2014). "The Impact of State Medical Marijuana Legislation on Adolescent Marijuana Use." *Journal of Adolescent Health* 55(2): 160–66. Available
at: https://pubmed.ncbi.nlm.nih.gov/24742758.

Cision. (2018). "Legal Marijuana Market Worth $146.4 Billion by 2025 |
CAGR: 34.6%: Grand View Research, Inc." April 30. Available at: https://
www.prnewswire.com/news-releases/legal-marijuana-market-worth-
1464-billion-by-2025--cagr-346-grand-view-research-inc-681217061.html.

Cision. (2021). "Legal Cannabis Market Size Worth $91.5 Billion by 2028 |
CAGR: 26.3%: Grand View Research, Inc." July 27. Available at: https://
www.prnewswire.com/news-releases/legal-cannabis-market-size-
worth-91-5-billion-by-2028--cagr-26-3-grand-view-research-inc-301341758
.html.

Collins, R. L., P. C. Vincent, J. Yu, L. Liu, and L. H. Epstein. (2014). "A Behavioral Economic Approach to Assessing Demand for Marijuana." *Experimental and Clinical Psychopharmacology* 22(3): 211–21. Available at: https://doi.org/10.1037/a0035318.

Cowen. (2020). "Themes 2020: Cannabis." February 27. Available at: https://www.cowen.com/insights/themes-2020/cannabis.

Davenport, S. D., and J. P. Caulkins. (2016). "Evolution of the United States Marijuana Market in the Decade of Liberalization before Full Legalization." *Journal of Drug Issues* 46(4): 411–27.

Davis, G. C., and M. C. Espinoza. (1998). "A Unified Approach to Sensitivity Analysis in Equilibrium Displacement Models." *American Journal of Agricultural Economics* 80(4): 868–79. Available at: https://doi.org/10.2307/1244070.

Davis, G. C., and N. C. Kruse. (1993). "Consistent Estimation of Armington Demand Models." *American Journal of Agricultural Economics* 75(3): 719–23. Available at: https://doi.org/10.2307/1243578.

Diep, F. (2015). "The Science of Decriminalizing Drugs." *Popular Science*, February 2. Available at: www.popsci.com/science-decriminalize-legalize-drugs-marijuana-weed.

Downs, D., B. Barcott, and F. Corva. (2019). "Special Report: Debunking Dispensary Myths." Leafly. Available at: http://www.scgalliance.com/wp-content/uploads/2019/06/Debunking-Dispensary-Myths-FINAL-2.0.pdf.

Edgerton, D. L. (1997). "Weak Separability and the Estimation of Elasticities in Multistage Demand Systems." *American Journal of Agricultural Economics* 79(1): 62–79. Available at: https://doi.org/10.2307/1243943.

Erdbrink, T. (2021). "In Amsterdam, Getting High at Coffee Shops May Soon Be for Locals Only." *New York Times,* January 8. Available at: www.nytimes.com/2021/01/08/world/europe/amsterdam-marijuana-coffee-shops-tourists.html.

Eschker, E., J. Kaplan, J. Zender, F. Krissman, J. Meisel, and A. Silvaggio. (2018). "Proposed Regulations for Manufacturers of Adult-Use and Medicinal Cannabis: Standardized Regulatory Impact Assessment (SRIA)." Prepared for the California Department of Public Health by the Humboldt Institute for Interdisciplinary Marijuana Research. Available

at: https://hiimr.humboldt.edu/sites/default/files/california_department_
of_public_health_april_2018-_sria_prop_64_-_joshua_zender.pdf.

George, P.S., and G.A. King. (1971). "Consumer Demand for Food Commodities in the United States with Projections for 1980." AgEcon Search.
Available at: https://doi.org/10.22004/ag.econ.11936.

Gold, R. (2018). "Harvard Quietly Amasses California Vineyards—and the
Water Underneath." *Wall Street Journal,* December 10. Available at:
https://www.wsj.com/articles/harvard-quietly-amasses-california-
vineyardsand-the-water-underneath-1544456396.

Goldstein, R. (2008). *The Wine Trials.* New York: Workman.

Goldstein, R. (2019). "Half-Blind Tasting: A Deception-Free Method for Sizing
Placebo and Nocebo Responses to Price and Packaging Attributes." *Journal
of Wine Economics* 14(3): 321-31. Available at: https://doi.org/10.1017/jwe
.2019.40.

Goldstein, R., J. Almenberg, A. Dreber, J.W. Emerson, A. Herschkowitsch,
and J. Katz. (2008). "Do More Expensive Wines Taste Better? Evidence
from a Large Sample of Blind Tastings." *Journal of Wine Economics* 3(1):
1-9. Available at: https://doi.org/10.1017/S1931436100000523.

Goldstein, R., R. Saposhnik, and D.A. Sumner. (2020). "Prices of Cannabis in
California from Licensed and Unlicensed Retailers." *ARE Update* 23(3): 1-4.
University of California Giannini Foundation of Agricultural Economics.
Available at: https://giannini.ucop.edu/publications/are-update/issues
/2020/23/3/prices-of-cannabis-in-california-from-licensed-and.

Goldstein, R., and D.A. Sumner. (2019). "California Cannabis Regulation: An
Overview." *California Agriculture* 73(3-4): 101-2. Available at: https://
escholarship.org/uc/item/3z46c37x.

Goldstein, R., D.A. Sumner, and A. Fafard. (2019). "Retail Cannabis Prices in
California through Legalization, Regulation and Taxation." *California
Agriculture* 73(3-4): 136-45. Available at: https://escholarship.org/uc/item
/30j3p1sg.

Gray, R.S., D.A. Sumner, J.M. Alston, H. Brunke, and A.K.A. Acquaye. (2005).
"Economic Consequences of Mandated Grading and Food Safety Assur-
ance: Ex Ante Analysis of the Federal Marketing Order for California
Pistachios." University of California Giannini Foundation of Agricultural
Economics, Monograph 46. Available at: https://s.giannini.ucop.edu

/uploads/giannini_public/5f/65/5f651bff-93e6-47a4-b0b2-38757c3a3294
/46_pistachios.pdf.

Gregory, M., S. Davenport, J. P. Caulkins, and B. Kilmer. (2019). "What
America's Users Spend on Illegal Drugs, 2006–2016." *RAND Research
Reports* RR-3140. Available at: https://www.rand.org/content/dam/rand
/pubs/research_reports/RR3100/RR3140/RAND_RR3140.pdf.

Grossman, M., and F. J. Chaloupka. (1998). "The Demand for Cocaine by
Young Adults: A Rational Addiction Approach." *Journal of Health
Economics* 17(4): 427–74. Available at: https://doi.org/10.1016/s0167-
6296(97)00046-5.

Gustafson C., T. J. Lybbert, and D. A. Sumner. (2016). "Consumer Sorting
and Hedonic Valuation of Wine Attributes: Exploiting Data from a Field
Experiment." *Agricultural Economics* 47(1). Available at: https://
onlinelibrary.wiley.com/doi/abs/10.1111/agec.12212.

Herron-Wheeler, A. (2021). "Cannabis Smoking Lounges Finally Approved
by Denver City Council." *High Times,* April 22. Available at: https://
hightimes.com/news/denver-cannabis-smoking-lounges.

Holowach, J., dir. (2008). *High: The True Tale of American Marijuana.* Holowach
Films.

Jacobi, L., and M. Sovinsky. (2016). "Marijuana on Main Street? Estimating
Demand in Markets with Limited Access." *American Economic Review*
106(8): 2009–45. Available at: https://doi.org/10.1257/aer.20131032.

Kilmer, B., J. P. Caulkins, G. Midgette, L. Dahlkemper, R. J. MacCoun, and
R. Liccardo Pacula. (2013). "Before the Grand Opening: Measuring
Washington State's Marijuana Market in the Last Year before Legalized
Commercial Sales." *RAND Research Reports* RR-466. Available at: https://
www.rand.org/pubs/research_reports/RR466.html.

Kilmer, B., J. P. Caulkins, R. Pacula, R. MacCoun, and P. Reuter. (2010).
"Altered State? Assessing How Marijuana Legalization in California Could
Influence Marijuana Consumption and Public Budgets." Available at:
https://doi.org/10.7249/OP315.

Lakhdar, C. B., N. G. Vaillant, and F. C. Wolff. (2016). "Price Elasticity of
Demand for Cannabis: Does Potency Matter?" *Addiction Research and
Theory* 24(4): 300–312. Available at: https://doi.org/10.3109/16066359.201
6.1139699.

Lexico, Oxford English Dictionary. (2021). "Enjoyment"; "Recreational."
    Retrieved August 7. Available at: https://www.lexico.com/definition
    /enjoyment; https://www.lexico.com/definition/recreational.
Lynne-Landsman, S. D., M. D. Livingston, and A. C. Wagenaar. (2013).
    "Effects of State Medical Marijuana Laws on Adolescent Marijuana Use."
    American Journal of Public Health 103(8): 1500–1506. Available at: www
    .ncbi.nlm.nih.gov/pmc/articles/PMC4007871.
MacCoun, R., and P. Reuter. (2001). "Evaluating Alternative Cannabis
    Regimes." *British Journal of Psychiatry* 178(2): 123–28. Available at: https://
    pubmed.ncbi.nlm.nih.gov/11157425.
MacEwan, D., D. Newman, R. E. Howitt, J. Noel, and M. Driver. (2017).
    "Economic Impact Analysis of CalCannabis Cultivation Licensing Program
    Regulations." Standardized Regulatory Impact Assessment (SRIA). ERA
    Economics LLC. Available at: https://www.dof.ca.gov/Forecasting
    /Economics/Major_Regulations/Major_Regulations_Table/documents
    /Cultivation_SRIA_CDFA_1–5-2018.pdf.
Marijuana Policy Group. (n.d.). "Marijuana in Colorado." Prepared for the
    Colorado Department of Revenue. Available at: https://www.colorado
    .gov/pacific/sites/default/files/Market%20Size%20and%20Demand%
    20Study,%20July%209,%202014%5B1%5D.pdf.
Matthews, W. A., D. A. Sumner, J. Medellín-Azuara, and T. Hanon. (2017).
    "Economics of the California Cut Flower Industry and Potential Impacts
    of Legal Cannabis." University of California Agricultural Issues Center.
    Available at: http://www.cafgs.org/assets/docs/final_calflower_report-
    web.pdf.
Merriam-Webster Collegiate Dictionary. (2021). Online ed. "Recreational."
    Retrieved August 7. Available at: https://www.merriam-webster.com
    /dictionary/recreational.
Miguel, K., and R. Aqui. (2018). "Legal Cannabis Lounges Booming in
    San Francisco." ABC7 San Francisco, December 18. Available at:
    https://abc7news.com/pot-cannabis-marijuana-pot-dispensary
    /4922997.
Miron, J. A. (2010). "The Budgetary Implications of Drug Prohibition."
    Department of Economics, Harvard University. Available at: https://
    scholar.harvard.edu/files/miron/files/budget_2010_final_0.pdf.

Muth, R.F. (1964). "The Derived Demand Curve for a Productive Factor and the Industry Supply Curve." *Oxford Economic Papers* 16(2): 221–34. Available at: https://www.jstor.org/stable/2662270.

Nisbet, C.T., and F. Vakil. (1972). "Some Estimates of Price and Expenditure Elasticities of Demand for Marijuana among U.C.L.A. Students." *Review of Economics and Statistics* 54(4): 473–75. Available at: https://doi.org /10.2307/1924578.

Orens, A., M. Light, J. Rowberry, J. Matsen, and B. Lewandowsky. (2015). "Marijuana Equivalency in Portion and Dosage." Colorado Department of Revenue. Available at: https://www.colorado.gov/pacific/sites/default /files/MED%20Equivalency_Final%2008102015.pdf.

Ours, J.C. van, and J. Williams. (2007). "Cannabis Prices and Dynamics of Cannabis Use." *Journal of Health Economics* 26(3): 578–96. Available at: https://doi.org/10.1016/j.jhealeco.2006.10.001.

Pacula, R.L., M. Grossman, F.J. Chaloupka, P.M. O'Malley, L.D. Johnston, and M.C. Farrelly. (2001). "Marijuana and Youth." In *Risky Behavior among Youths: An Economic Analysis,* National Bureau of Economic Research (NBER), 271–326. Available at: https://ideas.repec.org/h/nbr /nberch/10691.html.

Pacula, R.L., and R. Smart. (2017). "Medical Marijuana and Marijuana Legalization." *Annual Review of Clinical Psychology* 13:397–419. Available at: https://www.ncbi.nlm.nih.gov/pmc/articles/PMC6358421.

Pouliot, S., and D.A. Sumner. (2008). "Traceability, Liability, and Incentives for Food Safety and Quality." *American Journal of Agricultural Economics* 90(1): 15–27. Available at: https://www.jstor.org/stable/30139488.

RAND Corporation. (2009). "Drug Policy Research Center (DPRC) Insights." Available at: www.rand.org/well-being/justice-policy/centers/dprc /newsletter/2009/12.html.

Reinarman, C. (2009). "Cannabis Policies and User Practices: Market Separation, Price, Potency, and Accessibility in Amsterdam and San Francisco." *International Journal on Drug Policy* 20(1): 28–37. Available at: https://doi.org/10.1016/j.drugpo.2007.11.003.

Saitone, T.L., R.J. Sexton, and D.A. Sumner. (2015). "What Happens When Food Marketers Require Restrictive Farming Practices?" *American Journal of Agricultural Economics* 97(4): 1021–43. Available at: https://

farmdocdaily.illinois.edu/2015/09/what-happens-when-food-marketers-
require.html.

Savchuk, K. (2016). "Billionaire Sean Parker Wins, Sheldon Adelson Loses
on Marijuana Ballot Measures." *Forbes,* November 9. Available at: www
.forbes.com/sites/katiasavchuk/2016/11/09/billionaire-sean-parker-
wins-sheldon-adelson-loses-on-marijuana-ballot-measures/?sh=
1b4e470d1724.

Scarboro, M. (2017). "How High Are Marijuana Taxes in Your State?" Tax
Foundation. Available at: https://taxfoundation.org/marijuana-taxes-state.

Schroyer, J. (2015). "California Marijuana Leaders Increasingly Uniting
behind One Legalization Measure." *MJBizDaily,* December 10. Available
at: https://mjbizdaily.com/california-cannabis-leaders-increasingly-
uniting-behind-one-legalization-measure.

Schroyer, J. (2020). "Proposed Regulatory and Tax Reforms in California
Could Make Life Simpler for Marijuana Businesses." *MJBizDaily,* January
16. Available at: https://mjbizdaily.com/proposed-regulatory-and-
tax-reforms-in-california-could-make-life-simpler-for-marijuana-
businesses.

Stigler, G. (1971). "The Theory of Economic Regulation." *Bell Journal of
Economics and Management Science* 2(1): 3–21. Available at: https://www
.jstor.org/stable/3003160.

Substance Abuse and Mental Health Services Administration. (2014). "Results
from the 2013 National Survey on Drug Use and Health: Summary of
National Findings." NSDUH Series H-48, HHS Publication No. (SMA)
14-4863. Substance Abuse and Mental Health Services Administration.
Available at: https://www.samhsa.gov/data/sites/default/files
/NSDUHresultsPDFWHTML2013/Web/NSDUHresults2013.pdf.

Sumner, D. A., R. Goldstein, H. Lee, W. A. Matthews, Q. Pan, J. Medellin-
Azuara, T. Hanon, P. Valdes-Donoso, H. Lee, and J. Lapsley. (2018).
"Economic Costs and Benefits of Proposed Regulations for the Imple-
mentation of the Medicinal and Adult Use Cannabis Regulation and
Safety Act (MAUCRSA): Standardized Regulatory Impact Analysis."
Prepared for the California Bureau of Cannabis Control by the University
of California Agricultural Issues Center and submitted to the California
Department of Finance. Available at: www.dof.ca.gov/Forecasting

/Economics/Major_Regulations/Major_Regulations_Table/documents
/DCA Cannabis_SRIA_2018.pdf.

Sumner, D. A., R. S. Goldstein, W. Matthews, and O. Sambucci. (2020). "Legal
and Illegal Cannabis in California: An Overview after Two Years of
Taxation and Regulation." In *California Agriculture: Dimensions and Issues*,
Chapter 13. Berkeley, CA: Giannini Foundation. Available at: https://s
.giannini.ucop.edu/uploads/pub/2021/01/21/chapter_13_cannabis_2020
.pdf.

U.S. Department of Justice. (2017). "Union Organizer Indicted for Corrup-
tion, Attempted Extortion, and Money Laundering." September 17.
Available at: https://www.justice.gov/usao-ndca/pr/union-organizer-
indicted-corruption-attempted-extortion-and-money-laundering.

Valdes-Donoso, P., D. A. Sumner, and R. Goldstein. (2019). "Costs of
Mandatory Cannabis Testing in California." *California Agriculture*
73(3–4): 154–60. Available at: https://www.researchgate.net/publication
/335768737_Costs_of_mandatory_cannabis_testing_in_California.

Valdes-Donoso, P., D. A. Sumner, and R. Goldstein. (2020). "Costs of
Cannabis Testing Compliance: Assessing Mandatory Testing in the
California Cannabis Market." *PLOS One* 15(4): e0232041. Available at:
https://doi.org/10.1371/journal.pone.0232041.

Veblen, T. (1899). *The Theory of the Leisure Class: An Economic Study of
Institutions*. New York: Macmillan. Available at: https://www.gutenberg
.org/ebooks/833.

Von Lampe, K., M. Kurti, J. Johnson, and A. F. Rengifo. (2016). "'I Wouldn't
Take My Chances on the Street': Navigating Illegal Cigarette Purchases in
the South Bronx." *Journal of Research in Crime and Delinquency* 53(5):
654–80. Available at: https://doi.org/10.1177/0022427816637888.

Wall Street Journal. (2020). "California Deems Pot an Essential Coronavirus
Business." Staff Editorial. March 24. Available at: https://www.wsj.com
/articles/california-deems-pot-an-essential-coronavirus-business-
11585005903.

Weedmaps data. Available at: http://weedmaps.com.

Wohlgenant, M. K. (2001). "Marketing Margins: Empirical Analysis." In
Handbook of Agricultural Economics, Part 2, 933–70. Amsterdam: Elsevier.
Available at: https://ideas.repec.org/h/eee/hagchp/2-16.html.

Index

ballot measures (questions) *(continued)* 114, 120; on state weed legalization, 145. *See also* Proposition 19; Proposition 64; Proposition 215

banking system, weed business access restrictions to, 143–44, 146

beer, ix, 20, 57, 115; late-night weed and, 69; on-premise sale of, 63, 68; risk premium absence for, 47

Berkeley Patients' Group (BPG), 124

blunt, 62

Boehner, John, viii

Booth, Martin, 4, 5, 7

Boyd, Graham, 112

BPG. *See* Berkeley Patients' Group

British Columbia, Canada: greenhouse cultivation in, 148; tomatoes production in, 148–49

Brown, Jerry, 104

Brown Doctrine, 104–6

brownies, 25, 40, 55

Cabernet Sauvignon, 154

CAGR. *See* compound annual growth rate

California, vii, ix, 11–12, 118–21; ballot questions in, 16, 21, 45, 107–8, 110–12; Cannabis Event Organizer License, 68–69; Chardonnay, vapes, and spliffs in, 106; cultivation tax in, 49, 51; excise taxes in, x; farm prices in, 82*tab.*; Harvard University land investment and sales, 155–56; high and low prices in, 87; illegal weed growth in, 149; indoor large-scale legal production in, 148, 149;

late-night sales curfew in, 69, 70*fig.*, 71; medical collectives, 105–6; medical weed 8 ounce possession, 8; medical weed industry in, 110, 114–17; medical weed legalization, 101–3; opium crackdown in, 13; outdoor cultivation in, 84, 148; overall sales in, 96–98, 97*fig.*; recreational weed legalization in, 13, 18, 68–69; retailers in, 76*tab.*; retail prices in, 82*tab.*, 87, 88*tab.*; taxes impact on weed retail price in, 49–51, 50*tab.*; tomatoes production in, 148–49; 2022 low-end retail prices in, 161; Washington cheap legal weed and, 171–72; weed 1913 prohibition in, 13; Weedmaps listings in, 73, 129, 130*fig. See also* Proposition 19; Proposition 64; Proposition 215

Canada: Alberta production and processing, 167; British Columbia, 148–49; illegal weed in, 16; legalization in, 22, 166–67; legal weed 2050 trade, 139; legal weed compliance standards in, 45; Saskatchewan, 151; Weedmaps listings in, 74; wholesale distributor requirement in, 41

Cannabis (Booth), 4

Cannabis Benchmarks, data from, 73

Cannabis Event Organizer License, 68–69

Cannabis indica plant: Google searches for, 1–2, 3*fig.*; Lamarck naming of, 4; with 0.3 percent THC as hemp, 6

Cannabis sativa plant: Google searches for, 1–2, 3*fig.*; Linnaeus naming of, 4
capital expenditures, for indoor cultivation, 39
Carlyle, Thomas, ix, 164
carrots, 9, 155
Caulkins, Jonathan, 153
CCPR. *See* Coalition for Cannabis Policy Reform
Chardonnay, 106
climates, for outdoor cultivation, 84, 96; 148
Coalition for Cannabis Policy Reform (CCPR): Boyd separation from, 112; Gieringer of, 108, 109, 110, 118; Parker and, 118; ReformCA initiative campaign, 110
cocaine, 7, 13
coffeeshops: Amsterdam culture of, 65, 107; in Netherlands, 63–64; weed on-premise sale in, 63, 68
Cole Memo, on federal government raids end, 105
collectives, 127; Brown Doctrine on, 104; California medical, 105–6; nonprofit organization of, 105–6; Proposition 215, 102–3; SP 420 authorization of, 102
Colorado: farm prices in, 81, 82*tab.*; late-night sales curfew in, 69; light regulations in, 150; medical weed legalization in, 17; overall sales in, 96–98, 97*fig.*; recreational weed legalization in, 13, 18, 21, 108; retailers in, 76*tab.*; retail prices in, 82*tab.*, 88*tab.*; THC

potency in, 82; wholesale prices in, x
Commerce Clause, on weed interstate market, 144, 145–46, 173
commercial sales, SB 420 lack of regulation for, 102
Compassionate Use Act. *See* Proposition 215
compound annual growth rate (CAGR), in economic forecasting, 159
consumer: illegal weed lack of legal risk to, 24; legal or illegal weed choice, 25–26; Nelson and Snoop Dogg as, 30; weed quality and price for, 24–25
Controlled Substances Act (1970), 16; pharmaceutical industry boost from, 19; on weed as Schedule I narcotic, 14, 142–43
cooperatives: Brown Doctrine on, 104; California medical, 105–6; nonprofit organization of, 105–6; SP 420 authorization of, 102
corn, 36, 154
Costco, 152, 156
COVID-19: lockdowns affect on weed sales, 98–100, 99*fig.*; on-premise sales impacted by, 63, 64
Craft Weed (Stoa), 156–57
cultivation tax, in California, 49, 51
cut-flower business. *See* flowers, cut

dab rigs, 115
Dale Sky Jones, 107, 110, 112
Daschle, Tom, vii–viii
DEA. *See* Drug Enforcement Administration

DeAngelo, Steve, 110, 118
delivery service, by retailers, 115,
    119–20
demand curve, 27–29; for Oklahoma
    illegal retail weed, 33–34, 34*fig.*; for
    Oklahoma legal retail weed, 31–33,
    34*fig.*, 35; for Oklahoma retail
    weed, 29*fig.*, 30–31
Department of Justice (DOJ), on
    in-state weed sales, 147
dismal, ix, 164, 182
dispensary, 12, 57; of BPG, 124; Brown
    Doctrine and, 105; California,
    18, 105; DeAngelo founder of
    Oakland, 110; Oklahoma medical,
    96; SB 420 and, 103
distribution, of weed, 10; California
    high cost of, 83; costs of, 160;
    geographical, 167; price data on,
    80; Proposition 64 and, 116;
    Proposition 215 and, 101; steps of,
    83; technology and, 152; U.S. and
    Canada requirement of wholesale,
    41
DOJ. *See* Department of Justice
Dosist, 57, 60, 60*fig.*
DPA. *See* Drug Policy Alliance
Drug Enforcement Administration
    (DEA), Schedule I illegal narcotics
    removal by, 143
Drug Policy Alliance (DPA), 111–12,
    114

economic beneficiaries, of interstate
    commerce, 149–50
economic effects, 95; of imprison-
    ment, 133; of recreational weed
    legalization, 137–38

economic forecasting: on CAGR,
    159; of market revenue, 159;
    market size and, 158
ecstasy. *See* MDMA
Ehrlichman, John, 14
elasticity: of demand, 30; of supply,
    30–31
evangelical church, Proposition 19
    opposition by, 108
excise tax: California raising of, x;
    retail prices and, 37, 74, 119;
    wholesale prices and, 49, 50*tab.*
extraction system, for weed, 164*fig.*

farm cultivation: of almonds and
    alfalfa, 36, 150, 160; distribution of
    weed and, 41; equity relative to
    debt in, 156; interstate, interna-
    tional commerce and legal weed,
    150–51; prices, 28, 36; weed
    growing and selling expense, 37–38
farm prices, 82*tab.*, 83–84, 83*fig.*,
    162*tab.*, 163; of Oklahoma flower,
    90, 92; potency correlation with,
    82; taxes impact on, 50*tab.*, 61; ter-
    minology of, 81; of Washington
    flower, 88; Weedmaps on, 81
federal government raids, Cole
    Memo on, 105
federal legalization: DEAs Schedule
    I illegal narcotics removal, 143;
    without federal regulation, 143–44
federal regulation: federal legaliza-
    tion without, 143–44; on licensing,
    taxes, and standards, 143, 144;
    national legalization and, 170–71
Fendrick, Sabrina, 125*fig.*; back-
    ground of, 124; on cannabis and

taxation policy regulations, 132; on local control, 126–27; NORML newsletters by, 122; on Proposition 64, 124, 126; story of, 122–38

Florida, 76*tab.*

flowers, cut, 38, 54; farm prices for, 88, 90, 92; illegal and legal similarities in, 23–24, 23*fig.*; joint or spliff smoking of, 55; smokable form of, 1, 2*fig.*

$40 standard, for weed, 53–54, 79–80

geographic weed distribution, 167

Gieringer, Dale, 13; CCPR and, 108, 109, 110, 118; on DPA, 111; of NORML, 107, 108, 110, 131; on Proposition 19, 108, 110; on Proposition 64 public ban, 131

Ginsburg, Ruth Bader, 146

Gonzales v. Raich, 146–47

Google searches, for weed, cannabis, marijuana, 1–2, 3*fig.*

Grand View Research, on San Francisco retail markets, 141

greenhouse cultivation, 37, 84, 153; in British Columbia, 148; higher prices from, 38; technology in, 154

greenhouses, 29; benefits of, 38; technology on, 156

gummies, 19, 25, 56, 115

Harrison Act, 13

Harvard University: California land investment and sales, 155–56; Gieringer and, 109; Harvard MBA, 46; private equity individuals of, 134

Hawaii: indoor and greenhouse cultivation in, 149; medical weed legalization in, 17; retail prices in, 88, 88*tab*, 91

hemp, 2, 3, 62; Saskatchewan industrial market in, 151; weed compared to, 5–6

heroin, 7

Humboldt County, California: illegal weed production in, 43, 128; medical weed and, 43–44; national legalization impact on, 171

illegal arbitrage, 90, 161

illegal weed: California growth of, 149; in Canada, 16; consumer lack of legal risk for, 24; costs compared to legal weed costs, 52–54; criminal sale of, 24; flowers similarities to legal weed, 23–24, 23*fig.*; Humboldt County production of, 43; legal weed compared to, 23–26; local control positive impact on, 127; lower cost of, ix–x; picture of, 23*fig.*; by supplier, 128; 2050 cheaper cost projections, 166, 167; wholesale marketing cost of, 42, 47

Illinois: farm prices in, 81, 82*tab.*; outdoor cultivation in, 84; retailers in, 76*tab.*; retail prices in, 82*tab.*, 87, 88*tab.*, 91; THC potency in, 82

imprisonment: economic effects from, 133; for legal weed production and sales, 132, 133*fig.*; from Nixon War on Drugs, 122–23; risk

imprisonment *(continued)*
premium and, 47; for weed
possession, 120; weed possession
racial inequality, 15–16, 122; from
weed prohibition, 133. *See also*
prisoners
indica. See Cannabis indica
indoor cultivation, 38, 84; California
large-scale legal, 148, 149; kind
bud grade in, 56; large capital
expenditures for, 39; legal weed
costs from, 44–45; in Oklahoma,
30; technology and, 153–54, 163
ingestion forms of weed, 1
in-state commerce: DOJ on, 147;
medical weed legalization and,
147
international policy, of weed
prohibition, 14–15
international trade: arbitrage-based
price declines, 151; imports
blocked in, 176; legal weed farm
cultivation and, 150–51; of legal
weed in 2050, 139; local standards
and, 173; Nixon weed prohibition
in, 14; in tomatoes, 151–52; of
weed business, 142, 145, 147–52
interstate commerce, 162*tab.*;
arbitrage-based price declines, 89,
91, 151, 161; California and, 148,
150; Commerce Clause on, 144,
145–46; economic beneficiaries of,
149–50; *Gonzales v. Raich* and,
146; illegal weed transporters, 43;
law enforcement against, 147;
legalization of, 148; legal weed
farm cultivation and, 150–51;
lower prices and, 160; national

weed market options and, 170–71;
retailers and, 152; state price
differences and, 81, 90–91; trade
barriers, 175; Washington and,
148; of weed business, 142, 145,
147–52, 170–71

kind bud, 56

Lamarck, Jean-Baptiste, 4
Las Vegas: late-night weed in, 69;
MedMen advertisement, 98*fig.*;
MJBizcon at, vii, viii*fig.*
late-night sales curfews, 68, 69–71,
70*fig.*
law enforcement: legalization and
stricter, 132–33, 133*fig.*; Proposition
19 opposition by, 108–9; Proposition 64 features for, 119
laws: aspirational, 134–36, 135*fig.*; on
psychoactive substances, 9;
recreational weed distinction in,
6; three strikes and you're out, 15
Lee, Richard, 107
legalization: Canada and, 22,
166–67; federal, 143–44; impacts
of, xi, 54–61; Michigan protests
for, 18*fig.*; for prisoners releases,
123–24; stricter law enforcement
and, 132–33, 133*fig.*; weed business
process from, 22–23. *See also*
medical weed legalization;
recreational weed legalization
legal risk premiums, 48
legal weed: arbitrage opportunities,
149; flowers similarities to illegal
weed, 23–24, 23*fig.*; illegal weed
compared to, 23–26; premiumiza-

marijuana, 16; cultivation, 101-2; with more than 0.3 percent THC as, 6; Reagan on, 12; terms of, 2-3. *See also* weed

Marijuana Medical Handbook (Gieringer), 109

Marijuana Tax Act (1937), 13

market price, 157, 158

market size, 79, 159, 184; economic forecasting and, 158; market price and, 158; state differences in, 97; by total retail revenue, 160, 162*tab.*, 163, 165, 168-69

Maryland, 76*tab.*, 88*tab.*

Massachusetts: farm prices in, 82*tab.*; interstate commerce and, 148; national legalization impact on, 171; outdoor cultivation in, 84; recreational weed legalization in, 13; retailers in, 76*tab.*; retail prices in, 82*tab.*, 87, *88*, 88*tab.*; THC potency in, 82; Washington cheap legal weed and, 171-72; weed 1911 prohibition in, 12-13; weed prices in, 147

MBA, 46, 156

MDMA (ecstasy), 7

medical alcohol, 10-11

medicalization, of weed, 7-12

Medical Marijuana Regulation and Safety Act (MMRSA), 124; Proposition 64 modeled from, 117, 118, 119

medical-only drugs, Adderall and Oxycontin as, 8

medical weed: California 8 ounce possession of, 8; Humboldt County and, 43-44; Oklahoma as medical only state, 92-96, 132; Proposition 215 for, 16-17; qualifying conditions for, 9; states systems of, 17-18, 46

medical weed industry, 7-10; in California, 110, 114-17; decline in, 11-12; gummies, 19, 25, 56, 115; ReformCA on, 116; tinctures and dap rigs, 115; vape pens, 39-40, 55-56, 106, 115

medical weed legalization: ballot questions (measures) on, 145; in California, 101-3; in-state commerce and, 147; states list with, 17-18, 46

medicine, Booth on cannabis plants in, 7

MedMen advertisement, in Las Vegas, 98*fig.*

Mellow Yellow coffeeshop, in Amsterdam, 63

methamphetamine (meth), 7

Mexico: full legalization impact on legal weed, 166-67; indoor cultivation regulation costs in, 149; legal weed 2050 trade, 139; retail illegal weed sales in, 151; Sonora, 167

Michigan: farm prices in, 82*tab.*; high and low prices in, 87; legalization protests in, 18*fig.*; outdoor cultivation in, 84; retailers in, 76*tab.*; retail prices in, 82*tab.*, 87, 88*tab.*

middleman markups, legal weed costs and, 50-51

milk, 10, 28, 39, 149, 185

Missouri: retailers in, 76*tab.*; retail prices in, 88*tab.*; THC oil price in, 91

MJBizCon, vii, viii*fig.*, 164*fig.*

MMRSA. *See* Medical Marijuana Regulation and Safety Act

Montana, 76*tab.*, 78, 88*tab.*

national legalization: federal regulations impact, 170–71; legal weed production elimination from, 170; states opt out allowance in, 171; weed business help from, 170–72, 182, 184–85

National Organization for the Reform of Marijuana Laws (NORML), 13; Fendrick newsletters, 122; Gieringer of, 107, 108, 110, 131; on imprisonment from War on Drugs, 122–23; Proposition 19 support by, 107; ReformCA relationship with, 114–15

national weed market, with interstate trade options, 170–71

Nelson, Willie, 30, 41

Netherlands: coffeeshops in, 63–64; drug policy in, 14, 15; spliffs in, 62

Nevada: farm prices in, 82*tab.*; medical weed legalization in, 17; overall sales in, 96–99, 97*fig.*; retailers in, 76*tab.*; retail prices in, 82*tab.* 88*tab.*

New Mexico, 76*tab.*, 88*tab.*

Newsom, Gavin, 112

New York, 76*tab.*

NIMBYs. *See* Not In My Backyard

Nixon, Richard: Controlled Substances Act of, 14, 16, 19, 142–43; War on Drugs of, 122–23

nonprofit organization, of collectives and cooperatives, 105–6

NORML. *See* National Organization for the Reform of Marijuana Laws

North America, legal weed market in, 16–21

Not In My Backyard (NIMBYs), Proposition 64 and, 126–27

Oaksterdam, Proposition 19 support by, 107

Obama, Barack, 14

off-premise sale, of alcohol, 63

oil cartridges, for vape pens, 55

Oklahoma, 78; farm prices in, 82*tab.*; illegal retail weed supply and demand curves, 33–34, 34*fig.*; indoor cultivation in, 30; legal retail weed supply and demand curves, 31–33, 34*fig.*, 35; as medical-only state, 92–96, 132; production and processing in, 167; retailers in, 76*tab.*; retail prices in, 82*tab.*, 91; retail weed supply and demand curves, 29*fig.*, 30–31; SQ 788, 93–94; weed business lower costs, 150; Willie Nelson and Snoop Dogg as weed consumers in, 30

on-premise sales: of alcohol, 63, 68; COVID-19 impact on, 63, 64; of weed in coffeeshops, 63, 68

opium, 7, 13

Oregon: farm prices in, 82*tab.*; high and low prices in, 87; medical weed legalization in, 17; overall sales in, 96–98, 97*fig.*; recreational weed legalization in, 13; retailers in, 76*tab.*; retail prices in, 82*tab.*, 87, 88, 88*tab.*, 91

organic products: cost of, 160; farming methods, 57; technology and, 154

outdoor cultivation, 36–38, 153; California, 148. 84; climates for, 84, 96, 148; of illegal weed, 43, 149; lower potency from, 174; retail prices for, 56, 84, 161, 172; in Washington, 172

out-of-state residents sales prohibition, SB 420 and, 104

Oxycontin, 8

Parker, Sean, 113*fig.*; ballot questions funding by, 114, 120; CCPR and, 118; DPA and, 112, 114; Newsom contributions from, 112; Proposition 64 support by, 112–14, 118–20

Pennsylvania, 76*tab.*, 91

pharmaceutical industry, 20; alcohol Prohibition permission to, 10; Controlled Substances Act boost in, 19; weed prohibitions support, 19

pharmacies, 13; prescription sales financial benefits, 19–20

potency: farm prices correlation with, 82; outdoor cultivation and lower, 174; THC, 82

premiumization, 56, 58–59*figs.*, 61, 174; Dosist, 57, 60, 60*fig.*; of weed brands, 57

prices: illegal, 126, 128, 136; legal, 126, 128, 136–37. *See also* farm prices; retail prices; wholesale prices

primary caregivers, Proposition 215 on possession and cultivation by, 101–2

prisoners: legalization for release of, 123–24; Proposition 64 and Parker on, 120; weed activists advocating on behalf, 110

Pritzker, Nicholas, 114

private equity: agribusiness and, 155; legal weed and, 134; in 2050 legal weed projections, 166, 168–69

production and processing, imprisonment for legal, 132, 133*fig.*

production and processing, in legal weed 2050 projections, 166; in Alberta, Canada, 167; awareness of out-of-state weed and local standards, 172, 176; local standards on out-of-state weed, 172, 173; local weed price premiums and out-of-state weed, 172, 175; regions for weed premium places, 172, 174; technology and weed farm, 142, 152–55

products: diversification of, 54–56; retailer lists of, 74–75. *See also* manufacturing products; organic products

in, 96–98, 97*fig.*; Weedmaps on retailer prevalence and size, 76*tab.*

Stigler, George, 11, 19

Stoa, Ryan, 156–57

substitution effect, 27

supply chain: documentation in, 45; improvements in, 153

supply curve, 27–29; for Oklahoma illegal retail weed, 33–34, 34*fig.*; for Oklahoma legal retail weed, 31–33, 34*fig.*, 35; for Oklahoma retail weed, 29*fig.*, 30–31

tax, 32, 136; calculations of, 51; cultivation, 49, 51; distributor payment of, 42; filing returns of, 44; income tax rules, 143; IRS liabilities, 143; rate, 49, 137; retail revenue percentage of, 119; revenue data, 96; state costs after, 52; state excise, 49, 119, 158; weed price plus, 81; weed prices after, 37

taxes: farm prices impact from, 50*tab.*, 61; federal on alcohol, 145; federal regulation on, 143, 144; on legal weed, 49–52, 50*tab.*; Proposition 64 on, 117, 119; on weed business, 71; wholesale prices impact from, 49, 50*tab.*

tea, 146, 160

technology: in greenhouse cultivation, 154; indoor cultivation and, 153–54, 163; weed farm and processing production in 2050, 142, 152–55

tetrahydrocannabinol (THC), 91; hemp with 0.3 percent, 6; main

weed psychoactive ingredient, 3; marijuana with more than 0.3 percent, 6; potency, 82; vape pens and oil of, 39–40, 55–56

Texas, 47, 84, 94, 96

THC. *See* tetrahydrocannabinol

Thiel, Peter, 114

Thomas, Clarence: on *Gonzales v. Raich*, 146; on *Standing Akimbo, LLC. et al. v. United States*, 146–47

three strikes and you're out laws, 15

three-tier system, of Proposition 64, 118

tinctures, 115

tobacco: recreational use of, 9; spliffs cut with, 55, 62, 106; weed retail services sale restrictions for, 62, 66, 67*fig.*

tomatoes: California, British Columbia production of, 148–49; international commerce in, 151–52

total retail revenue: economic forecasting of market, 159; in legal weed 2050 projections for fall in, 166, 168; legal weed pipe dreams for growth in, 182, 184; market size by, 160, 162*tab.*, 163, 165, 168–69

tourism, 64, 127, 130

track-and-trace system, in manufacturing, 40, 42

truffle, white, 37

UC Davis, 73, 156

The Union documentary, 9

United States: full legalization impact on legal weed, 166–67;

United States (continued)
wholesale distributor requirement
in, 41. See also national legalization; Prohibition, of weed

vape pens, 106, 115; replaceable oil
cartridges for, 55, 150; THC oil in,
39–40, 55–56
vaporizers, 55, 60–61, 61fig.
Veblen, Thorstein, 26
Vermont, 13, 94

Walgreen, Charles, 11
Walgreens, 11, 152
Walmart, 152, 156
War on Drugs, of Nixon, 122–23
Washington State, 11–12, 147; cheap
legal weed from, 171–72; farm
prices in, 82tab.; high and low
prices in, 87; interstate commerce
and, 148; late-night sales curfew
in, 69; light regulations in, 150;
medical weed legalization in, 17;
overall sales in, 96–98, 97fig.;
recreational weed legalization in,
13, 18, 21, 108; retailers in, 76tab.;
retail prices in, 82tab., 87, 88,
88tab., 91; wholesale prices in, x
weed: AMA on, 14; authors' first use
of, 176–80; COVID-19 lockdowns
affect on sales, 98–100, 99fig.;
extraction system, 164fig.; forms
of, 54–55; $40 standard for, 53–54,
79–80; Google searches for, 1–2,
3fig.; hemp compared to, 5–6;
history of, 4–5; ingestion forms of,
1; Malaysia death sentence for
possession of, 15; manufacturing

products from, 39–42, 55–56;
medicalization of, 7–12; prisoners
advocating by activists, 110; as
Schedule I narcotic, 14, 142–43;
smokable flower form, 1, 2fig.;
terminology for, 2–3; wine
similarity to, 40
weed business: banking system access
restrictions, 143–44, 146; international trade of, 142, 145, 147–52;
interstate commerce of, 142, 145,
147–52, 170–71; local control
prohibition of, 127; from national
legalization, 170–72, 182, 184–85;
Oklahoma lower cost for, 150;
processes from legalization for,
22–23; regulations and taxes on, 71
weed business survival strategies,
172; individual regions' development, 174; local standards on
out-of-state imports, 173; local
weed development, 175; weed
shipped into states local standards
awareness, 176
weed doctors, 103–4, 106
weed investors, vii–viii, 183. See also
private equity
weed lounges, San Francisco alcohol
and tobacco restrictions for, 64,
66–68, 67fig.
Weedmaps e-commerce website:
California listings in, 73, 129,
130fig.; Canada listings in, 74; cost
of, 73; on farm prices, 81; on
recreational states retailers,
77–79; retailer product lists in,
74–75; on retail prices, 73–74,
79–80; on state retailer prevalence

Founded in 1893,
UNIVERSITY OF CALIFORNIA PRESS
publishes bold, progressive books and journals
on topics in the arts, humanities, social sciences,
and natural sciences—with a focus on social
justice issues—that inspire thought and action
among readers worldwide.

The UC PRESS FOUNDATION
raises funds to uphold the press's vital role
as an independent, nonprofit publisher, and
receives philanthropic support from a wide
range of individuals and institutions—and from
committed readers like you. To learn more, visit
ucpress.edu/supportus.